CUISINE
GRAND-MERE

CUISINE GRAND-MERE

Traditional French Home Cooking

MARIE-PIERRE MOINE

TIME LIFE BOOKS

ALEXANDRIA, VIRGINIA

Time-Life Books is a division of Time Life Inc.
Time-Life is a trademark of Time Warner Inc. and affiliated companies.

TIME-LIFE INC.
CHAIRMAN AND CHIEF EXECUTIVE OFFICER: Jim Nelson
PRESIDENT AND CHIEF OPERATING OFFICER: Steven Janas
SENIOR EXECUTIVE VICE PRESIDENT AND CHIEF OPERATIONS OFFICER: Mary Davis Holt
SENIOR VICE PRESIDENT AND CHIEF FINANCIAL OFFICER: Christopher Hearing

TIME-LIFE BOOKS
PRESIDENT Larry Jellen
SENIOR VICE PRESIDENT, NEW MARKETS: Bridget Boel
VICE PRESIDENT, HOME AND HEARTH MARKETS: Nicholas M. DiMarco
VICE PRESIDENT, CONTENT DEVELOPMENT: Jennifer L. Pearce

TIME-LIFE TRADE PUBLISHING
VICE PRESIDENT AND PUBLISHER: Neil S. Levin
SENIOR SALES DIRECTOR: Richard J. Vreeland
DIRECTOR, MARKETING AND PUBLICITY: Inger Forland
DIRECTOR OF TRADE SALES: Dana Hobson
DIRECTOR OF CUSTOM PUBLISHING: John Lalor
DIRECTOR OF RIGHTS AND LICENSING: Olga Vezeris

CUISINE GRAND-MERE
DIRECTOR OF NEW PRODUCT DEVELOPMENT: Carolyn M. Clark
NEW PRODUCT DEVELOPMENT MANAGER: Lori A. Woehrle
SENIOR EDITOR: Linda Bellamy
DIRECTOR OF DESIGN: Kate L. McConnell
PROJECT EDITOR: Jennie Halfant
TECHNICAL SPECIALIST: Monika Lynde
DESIGN ASSISTANT: Jody Billert

Text © Marie-Pierre Moine 1990, 2001

Printed in Portugal
10 9 8 7 6 5 4 3 2 1

School and library distribution by Time-Life Education, P.O. Box 85026, Richmond, Virginia 23285-5026.

Library of Congress Cataloging-in-Publication Data available upon request:
Librarian, Time-Life Books
2000 Duke Street
Alexandria, Virginia 22314

ISBN 0-7370-2067-9

Contents

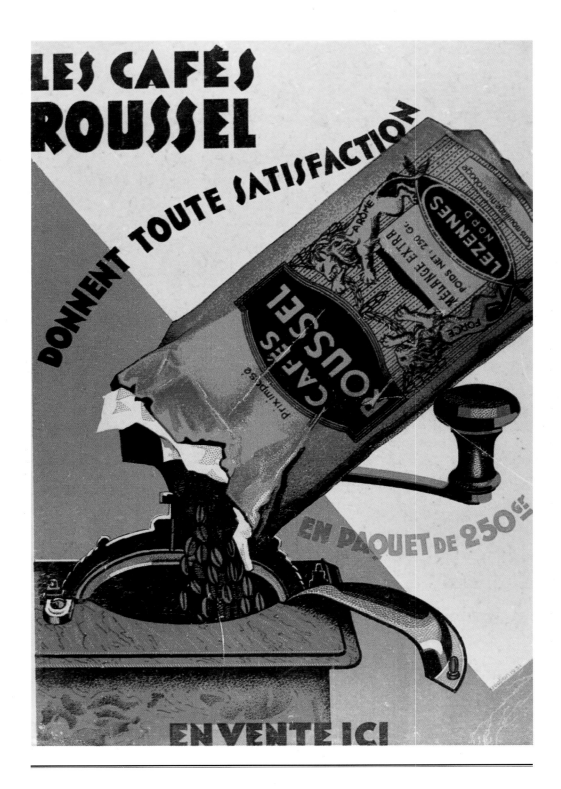

SOME OF MY happiest childhood memories are of my grandparents' kitchen at Fourchettes, their house near Amboise in the Loire valley. This is troglodyte country, the land of cave dwellers, and the Fourchettes kitchen was, in fact, such a cave, separate from the house, carved out of the rocks sixty feet beneath the wood that led up to the edge of the vineyards. The cave-kitchen was a magic place. It was empty of cheerful Fifties' gadgets, but full of mysteries, and large enough for us as small children to test our cycling skills around the old table when nobody was watching. It was cool in summer and mild in winter, with patches of green damp stubbornly coming up through the whitewash on the "walls."

I loved it for its strangeness and for the myriad good things that came from it. It was presided over by Madeleine, my grandmother's cook, who had been in the family much longer than I, and was my youngest aunt's godmother. She was the genius of the place, radiating good humor and energy. The grown-ups, after most meals, nodded their heads contentedly and commented without fail that she was "*vraiment une bonne cuisinière, une très, très, bonne cuisinière, une excellente cuisinière.*" I didn't have a great deal to compare Mado to, but, yes, her food tasted better than the food I normally ate, certainly much better than that I had at my parents' in Paris.

Like all magic places, the kitchen had its dangers. The huge black range that Mado kept constantly burning daunted me, a tame volcano on one side of the cave. On the other side was an ancient refrigerator so badly grounded that we children weren't allowed near it. I once disobeyed the rule and tried to open its door to steal an illicit *œuf à la neige*. It was siesta time and I was barefoot:; the shock was so violent that my aunt, who tried to prize me off, got stuck to the refrigerator too. Fortunately someone else made a dash for the fuse box and I live to tell the tale, wear sandals when raiding refrigerators, and still eat *œufs à la neige*.

The grass was greener on vacation, of course, but knowing that there was going to be a *tarte à l'oignon* or profiteroles for dinner added a glow to the afternoon. I always asked about the menu, helped pick for it in the garden, and reported faithfully to the kitchen most evenings after my bath, to tail beans and stir the vinaigrette, hoping to lick a few spoons here and there, while Madeleine, eyes watering from peeling onions, fed me family gossip, solved grievances, and explained why evaporated milk was better than cream in onion tart . . . . Nor was I the only one listening, for the kitchen was the newsroom and general refuge of the family—Mado knew everything, wasn't partisan, and dispensed sympathy, jokes, and common sense. She invariably had an audience around the oiled cloth of the central table while she hovered between the big kitchen range and the chipped enamel sink. More often than not, the adults present had a glass of "Fourchettes" wine in hand, to be concealed at once if my grandfather happened to walk in. That distinguished gentleman's pride and joy, the pick of his vineyard, his better bottles, so temptingly labeled "*pour les grandes occasions*" and more eminently drinkable than the ordinary wine he normally produced, had a habit of disappearing from his *cave*, the wine-cellar cave next door. His temper was formidable and we were terrified of it—very right, too: After all, it was his house. But the kitchen never really seemed to be under his jurisdiction.

Cuisine grand-mère is traditional French home cooking, the repertoire of dishes that are eaten *en famille* and as party pieces, recipes handed down from grandmother to mother to daughter, collected on scraps of paper from relations and friends. The principle remains the same, but the communication systems change with the times. My sisters and I are quickly getting into the habit of swopping recipes by fax, and Clémence, my 9-year-old niece, makes us all feel very old when she jots down a recipe dictated over the phone to try it for herself.

This book is about French home cooking as I know it—the way my family cooked. My *cuisine grand-mère* is based on family recipes that I started collecting, and experimenting with, nearly twenty years ago. Cooking proper began for me after leaving Oxford when I was let loose on my first kitchen in a basement flat in Shepherds Bush, a London neighborhood. My first graduate dinner party was a mitigated success. I scalded my ankle when I dropped a dish of braised celery (no one saw the mishap, so back into the dish went the wretched vegetable). The evening was saved by Madeleine's *pommes meringuées*, a gorgeous triple-layered combination of tart apple slices at the bottom, thick, sweet *crème pâtissière* in the middle, and crisp meringue on top.

Recipes in a family network are never particularly precise—a little glass of this and a handful of that, a pinch of this and two fingers' width of that—but battles can rage between relatives and friends about their different versions of the same dish. Do you really put mushrooms in your *bœuf bourguignon*, cheese in your *quiche lorraine*, croutons around your *blanquette de veau*? If the dish is a success, the argument is forgotten and the revised version of the recipe—or some particularly good trick—may make its way in due course into a new set of files.

Cuisine grand-mère is not about authenticity at all cost. It always errs on the side of practicality. It loves making do, with the help of little twists that work well, clever *trucs*, not-so-secret family secrets proudly and willingly shared with others. It assumes that the recipients are not absolute beginners, but have a clue about basic techniques, enough common sense, and a touch of flair. Given these not unreasonable assumptions, it is friendly and sensible, not aimed at experts, but at amateurs who have to cook regularly and might as well get some satisfaction from it.

Sometimes it will cut corners, especially when it comes to daunting complex classics with dozens of obscure ingredients. Sensible editing takes place: The chances are—outside the southwest of France—that a family *cassoulet* will not quite be the "real" thing, whatever that may be. But it will be practical and will probably taste all right even if you are hundreds of miles from the Castelnaudary market. Last but not least it will not be extravagant.

Thrift is an important part of the *grand-mère* approach. My own grandmother enjoyed telling us, three-quarters jokingly, that we were lucky to have both butter and jam on our *tartines*. It wasn't like that in her day, one or the other, yes, but not both. That was a matter of principle.

Cheaper cuts of meat are simmered for a long time, variety meat tackled uncompromisingly, vegetables and seasonal produce feature prominently when at their best and cheapest. I remember the astonishment on an American boyfriend's face when he was formally served a summer dinner of boiled egg (one or two, on request), followed by a mountain of *haricots verts* from the garden, tender, buttered,

The main approach to Fourchettes

and garlicky. Then came a local *Cendré* goat cheese and, at the last, a large dish of strawberries, picked that afternoon, served with *crème fraîche* in honor of our guest. He asked me if my grandmother was a vegetarian—this was in the early Seventies, before vegetarian became a household word.

In the Seventies and during most of the Eighties, poor old *cuisine grand-mère* took quite a knocking. It was eclipsed by the clean lines and sharp colors of *nouvelle cuisine*. It lost the battle in bistros and homes *à la mode* (*grand-mère*, in any case, never claimed to be the cuisine of top restaurants), but patiently waited for the wheel to turn and upstart *nouvelle* to lose its youthful charm. And, after two decades, the age of *cuisine grand-mère* has clearly come again. Fashionable chefs everywhere are confiding that they have rediscovered the joys and values of *cuisine traditionnelle* (the expensive, professional relative of both *grand-mère* and its fundamentalist country cousin, *cuisine du terroir*), while remembering the strong points of *nouvelle*—lightness, apparent simplicity, and the use of the best possible ingredients.

The good-natured *grand-mère* approach is nothing if not flexible. It has reacted well to this new challenge, lost a few calories, worked on its looks, and adopted some new tricks. Once again it is comfortably reigning in French kitchens—even if recipes have to be faxed during the cook's office hours.

Cuisine grand-mère is old-fashioned by definition. It assumes that the cook's place is in the house—not necessarily at the stove, but at hand: to give the pot a quick stir, add a few mushrooms twenty minutes before serving, then finish off the sauce with a nifty liaison. Rather than great skills, it requires a little attention and a presence. In the 1990s it makes perfect weekend cooking—relaxing but fiddly enough to be satisfying for the person who enjoys cooking. And it is ideal for the growing number of people who are choosing to work from home—what could be nicer than abandoning the desk for five minutes' creative puttering in the kitchen?

The end result will be satisfying, too: There is nothing particularly *légère* about *cuisine grand-mère*. I have tried to make my recipes as light as possible without altering their character and have given options whenever I can. This was not too difficult an exercise as, perhaps not altogether by accident, thrifty often coincides with healthy in the *grand-mère* style as I know it. First course salads and vegetables are used in abundance, and sweet desserts kept for special occasions. By tradition butter, cream, and eggs are ingredients you are supposed to be reasonably economical with. Flour I use sparingly. Waste not, want not: This is not stinginess, but just good old household management. The French spend a great deal more of their income on food than the Americans or English, but they believe in spending their money wisely.

One other cost-conscious lesson that I try to heed is to make leftovers palatable—I am not saying that I use them creatively, because the idea of stretching *les restes* to the limit makes me shudder. Old habits die hard, however. As I write I am recovering from a surfeit of leftover Easter *gigot*. It was a joy served cold at the next meal, with a good garlic mayonnaise, and still pretty good the day after as a spicy *hachis parmentier* under a layer of creamed potato. But what was I to do on the third day? There was still a lot of *gigot* left. Well, I hesitated and looked at it, and thought of stuffed tomatoes and hesitated again. In the end, the dog Dickie had a great supper.

A cave sitting room with frescoes

POSTSCRIPT

IT IS NOW ten years since I wrote *Cuisine Grand-Mère*. Looking back over the decade, I take stock of the spirit of the time. A passion for food and all things to do with food has swept the Western world, both old and new. Chefs have eclipsed photographers and hairdressers as media darlings, television stars, and gossip column fodder. My professional world of food magazine journalism has been hit by commercial realism. Anything to do with food must now have a spin, a marketing plan, or sponsors with deep pockets. (The concept of spin was unheard of in 1990: Let's hope that it is but a flash in the pan. In French a spinning top is a *toupie*, and *têtes de toupie*, people with heads like spinning tops, are notoriously dizzy and forgetful.) The age of culinary innocence may appear to be in danger of disappearing.

What most threatens culinary integrity in France is an epidemic of fast-food outlets. My 8-year-old niece Juliette, one of the aforementioned and now quite grownup Clémence's two little sisters, recently insisted on a McDonald's lunch after a morning's travels around London with a doting but unamused aunt. On her first visit to this strange big city, the red and yellow *M* shone like a reassuring beacon. She

Lotte à la Provençale

750 g de lotte
4 tomates ou 1 petite boîte
2 gros oignons
1 gousse d'ail
1 verre de vin blanc sec
6 cuillerées à soupe d'huile d'olive
50 g de fromage râpé
persil, thym, romarin, sel, poivre,

Coupez la lotte en morceaux. Faites-la revenir vivement à la poêle dans la moitié de l'huile d'olive avec l'oignon haché. Très vite la lotte deviendra plus ferme et d'un blanc doré. Retirez-la de la poêle, disposez-la dans un
T.S.V.P

Monkfish

Gratin dauphinois

750 g de p. de terre
2 oeufs
½ litre lait
2 gousses d'ail
sel, poivre
50 g de beurre

Coupez les p. de terre en rondelles assez fines. Disposez les par rangées dans un plat en terre, préalablement frotté avec une gousse d'ail puis beurré. Faites tiédir le lait, battez y les oeufs avec sel, poivre et une muscade, versez et mélangez sur les p. de terre. Ajoutez g. morceau de beurre la surface. Cuisez à four chaud environ 45 mn.

Potato gratin

Gratin de Haddock au riz

pour 4 personnes

750 g de filets de haddock
1 l de lait
50 g de fromage râpé
1 oeuf
250 g riz
sel, poivre, noix muscade, persil
50 g de beurre ou margarine
3 cuillerées de chapelure

Lavez les filets de haddock, mettez-les à cuire à l'eau froide. Quand l'eau commence à bouillir égouttez le haddock, remettez à cuire à l'eau froide. Laissez frémir 5 minutes, égouttez, rincez puis bien finir de dessaler. X Puis mettez à cuire le haddock dans 1 l. de lait avec une cuillerée de beurre et
T.S.V.P

Smoked haddock

just had to have *un apimil au Macdo* (a request that puzzled me until I worked out the phonetics; parents of young children will be quicker to spot the happy meal phenomenon).

Yet all is not gloom and doom, even if you surrender children under the age of ten to Ronald McDonald. Later in the day, young Juliette helped prepare a proper lemony cream sauce, to serve with salmon fillets roasted in the oven. She then did it full justice. The next generation, in France at any rate, seems to have the ability to enjoy both fast food and good home cooking–*cuisine grand-mère*. Different foods for different occasions. It helps enormously that family meals, less frequent because of the increasing pressure of work on both parents, are still an institution. These meals tend to be simpler than in the past during the working week–not just because of the pressure of time, but also because eating healthily has emerged as an everyday priority. On birthdays and high days and holidays, families still gather around a table to enjoy food, drink, and conversation. Calorie counts and fat contents are defied. Requests are made for what will be served at the next such occasion. Favorite dishes and past culinary triumphs are fondly evoked.

Mado's chocolate profiteroles, Tante Yonnée's lamb tagine, Anne-Sophie's terrines, Tata Boucher's sautéed potatoes . . . over the generations, my family goes on sharing a repertoire of dishes that entranced our taste buds and captured our imagination as children. Whenever I eat food prepared by my aunt, my sisters, or my cousins, there is always something uniquely familiar about it. In their hands even new recipes feel like old acquaintances. They are easy to remember and adopt. E-mails have replaced faxes (although not the backs of envelopes) as a means of swapping recipes, but we still speak the same culinary language. I am always surprised by how differently our generation, late thirties to just-turned fifty, rewrites our shared history. We remember the events and people of our childhood and adolescence very differently, but our foodie memories tend to be happy and have much in common. This must have a lot to do with the fact that our elders enjoyed their food, their wine, and the rituals of family meals. Tempers may have flared and opinions differed, usually about politics, but not until after the main course. I remember my uncle Denis storming out of the dining room during a heated summer lunch sometime during the De Gaulle era. His dramatic exit took him no farther than the kitchen, where he was soon found happily enjoying second helpings and a glass of wine, care of Mado the peacemaker.

Mado is now well into her eighties, indomitably independent and living near Limoges, a compulsory detour for any member of the family who happens to be traveling to the southwest of France. Despite bad arthritis, she still sends my aunt Noëlle, her goddaughter, a home-baked cake every Christmas. She has remained the cheerful confidante of the family. Just as I used to listen to her in the kitchen, I ring her for news and gossip and sometimes to clarify details of family history. She asks me for updates about life in London and about my husband Colin, whom she only met twice, but approved of as if she had known him forever because of his *sens de l'humor très british*. She is keen to know about vacations in Saint-Malo in Brittany, our new vacation home.

Our time in the Touraine came to an end when my father died. After the well-known riches of the produce of the Loire valley, the trips to farmhouses for goat cheese, the wine tastings at local producers, the familiar combinations of ingredients, the move to Saint-Malo was a complete break. It immediately rejuvenated my enthusiasm for traditional home cooking, and has resulted in a batch of new recipes in this book. It is a great joy and luxury to have a different local market to go to every day of the week. I write the names with a smile: Paramé, Dinard, Rocabey, Saint-Servan–they all offer fantastic fish and seafood, farmhouse poultry, and salt-marsh lamb. There is always one stall selling hand-churned salty butter, slapped into shape for each customer. The vegetables can require a lot of scrubbing, particularly the mushrooms and the tiny nutty potatoes stall holders tend to keep under the table for people who know what to ask for, but their flavor is well worth the elbow grease.

More often than not, the unpredictable climate of Saint-Malo means that the kitchen is the best place to spend an afternoon, closely observed by Muscade, my brother-in-law's glossy black Labrador, helped or not by occasional skilled, or not-so-skilled, willing *sous-chefs* of various ages. The kind of cooking I do there is not so much complicated as considered. I take time to blanch ingredients, flavor stocks, finely chop shallots and herbs, simmer sauces patiently. The idea is to make the ingredients sing, not a grand opera, but a jolly *chanson*. In the spirit of *cuisine grand-mère*, I try to prepare dishes we will all enjoy eating, and, who knows, dishes the next generation will remember.

beurre manié: mash together 1 teaspoon each of flour and soft butter. Divide into pellets and stir vigorously into hot sauces that need thickening over the heat.

butter: probably because I was brought up eating unsalted butter, I now really enjoy the taste of butter that is lightly salted. When a recipe does, however, demand soft unsalted butter, it is specified.

chicken stock: a light stock can easily be made by simmering the carcass, or at least some bones and gizzards, if possible, with a leek (or scallion), carrot, and bouquet garni (a sprig each of parsley and thyme and a bay leaf) for 30 minutes while you cook the meat. For a more elaborate method, see the *poule au pot* recipe (page 88). Chicken stock is worth having in the freezer.

chinois: a narrow strainer, extremely fine, and a useful utensil to have.

citrus fruit: buy organic or unwaxed lemons and oranges, especially if you are going to zest them. If time allows, blanch strips of zest for a minute in boiling water before using.

crème fraîche: heavy cream with a dash of lemon makes a most acceptable substitute.

eggs: I use organic or free-range eggs, keep them in the refrigerator, and ruthlessly throw away any unused eggs that are past their use-by date. And, without being pious about it, it is a good idea always to break eggs separately into a small bowl or saucer. The, albeit rare, occasions when an egg is bad invariably happen when you've just broken the last of the ten required for a mammoth meringue.

fish stock: the quickest of all stocks to make, with fish bones, shrimp, or other crustacean shells, simmered in water for 10 minutes with a bouquet garni. Avoid using the bones and trimmings of fatty fish such as salmon.

food processor: invaluable, particularly for non-pastry cooks, but takes a while to become second nature. I am still using my faithful old Magimix *Cuisine Système 3000,* and contemplating upgrading to a chrome-finish model I can leave permanently on display on the kitchen island. Choose a model that comes with a second smaller bowl, for everyday quick jobs.

garnish: I do not like the word. Think of it as a flourish; it should really add something to the dish—ideally a combination of zingy fresh flavor and visual appeal.

herbs: I use fresh herbs extravagantly, and try to grow my own—with mixed success I have to say. As well as growing herbs, supermarkets sell packed herbs in little trays. Look for herbs packed in deeper trays, with as distant a sell-by date as possible. Keep in the refrigerator, and cover with dampened paper towels after opening. Instead of letting them turn a stale yellow, finely chop leftover basil, parsley (including the stems), coriander, dill, chives, and tarragon, and freeze in tiny freezer bags. Shake out straight from the freezer as needed, and use again and again.

hollandaise sauce: I make mine in the food processor. Bring to a boil 4 teaspoons of white wine vinegar or lemon juice with 3 tablespoons of water. Season with freshly ground black pepper and reduce the mixture to about 2 teaspoons. Melt 10 tablespoons (150 g) unsalted butter in a separate saucepan until foamy—but do not let color. Process 2 egg yolks with a small pinch of salt until smooth. Whizz in the reduced vinegar. With the machine on, trickle in the bubbling butter through the feed tube, a few drops at a time to begin with then a little faster as the sauce starts to emulsify. Continue until the sauce is smooth and thick. Check the seasoning and use as soon as possible—or keep for up to 30 minutes over warm water.

kitchen hygiene: I use a separate chopping board for raw meat and go through vast amounts of paper towels and disposable kitchen clothes. Dishcloths are put in a very hot wash and tend to have a very short life.

lardons: now sold in supermarkets. If you cannot find packed lardons in the freezer section, look for diced pancetta. We French have a word for it, *ventrèche*—a perfect alternative to lardons. Otherwise, ask your local favorite delicatessen or butcher to sell you bacon in thick, 1-inch (2.5-cm) slices. Cut into small dice. The flavor and crunch they add to salads, quiches, and other dishes–lentils in particular–will be much greater than if you simply snip a standard bacon slice.

mayonnaise: hard-to-resist lovely mayonnaise can be made the slow painful way, by hand with a wooden spoon–or painlessly whizzed in the food processor. I tend to compromise with an electric mixer. Once you have made sure the ingredients and equipment are all at the same room temperature, and promised yourself that on no account will you speed up the process and pour in the oil too fast, there remains the familiar problem of having only two hands. One hand is to trickle in the oil, and the other to hold the mixer. But what about the slippery bowl? I wedge it firmly in place on a mat of damp kitchen cloth.

As much as I like olive oil, I do not recommend using it on its own for mayonnaise–it will completely take over. Peanut oil on its own is extremely bland, so I use the mix below.

Serves 6
2 egg yolks
2 teaspoons wine vinegar (red or white)
a small pinch of salt
½ teaspoon (8 g) Dijon mustard
⅔ cup (150 ml) peanut oil
½ cup (120 ml) light flavored olive oil
TO SEASON
freshly ground black pepper
sea salt
lemon juice
TO FLAVOR
finely chopped herbs–chervil, chives, parsley, tarragon, or watercress
finely chopped garlic
finely chopped gherkins
anchovy extract

BRING ALL THE INGREDIENTS AND EQUIPMENT TO room temperature.

Beat the egg yolks until combined, then beat in the vinegar, salt, and mustard. Whisking constantly, trickle in the peanut oil, literally drop by drop to begin, then a few drops at a time.

As soon as the mixture really appears to be thickening, trickle in the olive oil just a little more continuously, still whisking. Continue until you have incorporated both the peanut and olive oils.

Now taste the mayonnaise and season it with freshly ground black pepper, extra salt, if you like, and a little lemon juice. Beat in 1 tablespoon of boiling water, which will help the mayonnaise keep stable. Cover with plastic wrap and chill until needed. If you like, flavor to taste with some of the suggested additions.

measurements: these are expressed in American cups, with metric in parentheses. Follow only one set.

microwave: I have one, but it stays idle except for the odd reheating job. My one and only microwave

party trick is to use it to precook mushrooms before frying or roasting, to get rid of excess moisture. Put them in a microwave dish, cover loosely, and cook on high for 3 or 4 minutes. Drain well, and use as required. You will be pleasantly surprised by the taste and texture. It is also good for wilting tomatoes before you add them to omelets and other preparations. First pierce the skin or halve the tomatoes, then microwave, just like the mushrooms, for 2 or 3 minutes.

oil: for reasons of space, I limit the selection in my pantry. I keep sunflower oil, two kinds of olive oil, and an everyday blend with a light flavor for cooking; and for salads and last-minute dousing I use a gutsy, extra-virgin olive oil. There are many brands and styles to experiment with. Walnut oil I only buy in small bottles and store in the refrigerator–it goes rancid very quickly, so don't keep it longer than 3 months.

paper towels: use liberally for drying ingredients and wiping hands, utensils, and countertops.

peeling: in the recipes I assume that garlic and onions are peeled as a matter of course. If other vegetables require peeling, this is specified.

salad spinner: a wonderful gadget that collects all the moisture from salad leaves and saves a great deal of time and energy. A modest investment that I thoroughly recommend.

sauce blanche: white sauce. This quick recipe is a useful starting point for many variations. As well as the additions I suggest, also try mustard and capers. Béchamel sauce is made in exactly the same way, using milk instead of water. Flavor with tomato paste (purée) or cream and grated Gruyère cheese.

Serves 4
4 tablespoons (60 g) butter
4 tablespoons (60 g) flour
2¼ cups (550 ml) light stock or water
sea salt
freshly ground black pepper
TO ENRICH
2 tablespoons (30 g) or more butter, and/or the juice of 1 lemon
or ⅔ cup (150 ml) *crème fraîche*
or 1 egg yolk and 6 tablespoons light cream

IN A HEAVY-BOTTOMED SAUCEPAN, OVER A MODERATE heat, melt the butter, then stir in the flour, using a wooden spoon. Moisten at once with a little of the stock or water, stir to mix–from this stage on, I use a balloon whisk. Add the rest of the liquid, still stirring. Bring slowly to a boil, whisking very frequently, then reduce the heat and cook for several minutes–this is important, otherwise the sauce will taste floury. Season to taste with sea salt and freshly ground black pepper.

Enrich the sauce with 2 tablespoons (30 g) or more butter and the juice of 1 lemon, or with ⅔ cup (150 ml) *crème fraîche* just before serving. Alternatively, in a small bowl combine 1 large egg yolk

and 6 tablespoons light cream. Stir a little warm sauce into the egg and cream, then add to the pan and whisk in vigorously over the heat. Keep whisking hard until the sauce becomes creamy.

sauté pan: like all French home cooks I use mine a great deal.

scissors: I keep several pairs of kitchen scissors and use them constantly, for snipping fresh herbs, scallions, bacon slices, etc. In the interests of hygiene, the scissors used for snipping raw meats are a different color.

sea salt: it tastes better than ordinary salt and you need less of it. The texture of coarse kosher salt is particularly pleasant.

shortcuts: in my experience the French have always believed in using little tricks to make life easier and are no puritans when it comes to shortcuts in the kitchen. Convenience is not necessarily a dirty word. I use a lot of prepared salads, and I have to admit I sometimes buy chilled pastry and meat stocks: expensive, but money well spent when you are a gourmande in a hurry.

spatula: a good spatula should be heatproof and flexible. It is not an easy thing to find. The best one I ever had was a present from an American friend and I have never found its like in Britain or France.

things to bring back from France: the list varies from year to year. My current shopping list includes small blue-green *lentilles du Puy,* bitter dark chocolate, *saucisson,* small cans of extra-fine flageolets, *petits pois,* sugared ground almonds, tarragon mustard, caramels made with salted butter, and incredibly buttery miniature Britanny biscuits, to give to friends. I no longer bring back cheeses, because most will not mature well after a bout of traveling.

timing: I find that even if I follow a recipe to the letter, the exact timing mysteriously varies from one occasion to the next. Always keep an eye on the progress and be prepared to take action and turn the heat up, down, or off sooner–or later–than expected.

tomato *coulis:* a thin, strained purée of the juice and pulp of either canned or preferably fresh ripe tomatoes. *Coulis* is infinitely better than tomato paste (purée) and much used in the French kitchen–and mine.

vinaigrette: often too acidic. Use only top-quality vinegar and oil. A good basic vinaigrette is made with 1 tablespoon of red wine vinegar, 5 tablespoons of peanut oil, a tiny quantity of mustard, and a generous seasoning of sea salt and pepper. Stir vigorously with a small sauce whisk.

If like me, you eat large quantities of salad and like a thick and emulsified vinaigrette, follow my uncle Jean's method. Blend or process together 6½ tablespoons (100 ml) red wine vinegar, 2½ cups (600 ml) peanut oil, 1 tablespoon of strong Dijon mustard, 2 teaspoons of salt, and plenty of freshly ground black pepper. Check the seasoning and refrigerate for 1 hour, then blend or process again. Refrigerate in a tightly closed, impeccably clean jar. This vinaigrette will keep for up to 3 weeks.

vinegars: too many bottles crowd kitchen shelves and gather dust. Since a little vinegar goes a long way, buy the more expensive brands. I tend to keep a bottle or two of good wine vinegars, sherry vinegar, and balsamic and cider vinegars.

Potages
Soups

A LARGE WHITE CHINA tureen in the center of the table, fragrant steam, deep plates full of velvety goodness–my early memories of soup are of contentment and a feeling that things were as they should be and had always been. The curtains were drawn against the winter night, a clock was ticking somewhere. I was sharing an evening meal with my father's parents, *Bon-Papa* and *Bonne-Maman*, a quietly happy couple at peace with the world.

In France, as elsewhere, soup for a long time was the only dish at the last meal of the day. Hence the verb *souper*, which meant just what it said–to take evening soup–centuries before it went upmarket to describe a late, light meal. Soup in French homes has remained an evening rather than a lunchtime dish, appetizer, or main course, perhaps not quite as popular as it used to be, but making a distinct comeback now that more and more kitchens are equipped with that magic *robot*, the food processor. It seems that once again soup is good for you.

Soupe or *potage?* Most French people will tell you that the words are synonymous, but if you delve into it, *potage* turns out to be rather more refined, implying culinary skills, the use of a strainer, or the making of a liaison. Soup started life humbly as a slice of stale bread over which hot liquid was poured. It has remained part of the French experience every bit as much as cheese: Some decades ago Curnonsky listed more than five hundred varieties of *soupes* and *potages*, from starry kitchens to farmhouses.

Soup is flexible and accommodating–the only thing it does suffer from is not being served hot enough. As I like a good, substantial soup, but not buckets of it, I have generally allowed in the recipes about 5 cups (1.2 liters) liquid for 4 servings. This is only a guideline, as many factors influence the water content of any given vegetable. Feel free to vary and add a little extra water, stock, or cream if the soup seems too thick–or if you have an extra guest. Soup is a dish that can usually be stretched to go a little farther.

Potage au Potiron
Pumpkin Soup

WITH THE EXCEPTION of zucchini, the favored baby of the family, gourds and squashes do not feature very highly on the list of prized French vegetables. Pumpkins, in particular, have a lowly status and are often regarded as cattle fodder. However, they are discreetly put to very good use in a number of tasty, country-style soups, like my autumnal favorite here.

Serves 4

1 pound (450 g) wedge of
   pumpkin
2 large ripe tomatoes
1 large white onion
4 tablespoons (60 g) butter
1 scant tablespoon (10 g) sugar
5 cups (1.2 liters) milk
sea salt
freshly ground black pepper
4 tablespoons (60 ml) light
   cream
a few sprigs of parsley
croutons, to serve

REMOVE THE SKIN AND SEEDS FROM THE pumpkin, and dice the flesh. Blanch, skin, and seed the tomatoes, then chop the flesh. Coarsely chop the onion. In a large, heavy-bottomed saucepan, melt half the butter. Then stir in the vegetables and cook for a couple of minutes. Sprinkle in the sugar and add a small glass of water. Cover and cook gently for about 30 minutes, or until all the vegetables are soft.

Meanwhile, bring the milk to a boil in a suitable saucepan; keep hot. Add half the milk to the cooked vegetables and blend, using a blender or food processor, then pour the mixture into the pan with the remaining hot milk and whisk in. Alternatively, push the purée through a strainer into the hot milk and whisk in vigorously until well combined.

Season to taste with salt and freshly ground black pepper, then stir in the cream. Keep the soup hot over a gentle heat. Snip the parsley. Just before serving, whisk in the remaining butter.

Sprinkle the croutons and the snipped parsley over the soup and serve.

SOUPE AU PISTOU
Vegetable Soup with Basil, Garlic, and Cheese

Pistou is what Genoa's *pesto* becomes along the coast, on the French side of the border. This big, generous soup is well worth the entire crop of a kitchen pot of basil. Followed by a lightly dressed green salad, some cheese, and a little fruit, it makes a good *plat unique* supper. And it has the advantage of being unobtrusively vegetarian–a good dish to serve to a mixed party. The meat eaters won't miss their fix.

Serves 6 to 8

12 ounces (350 g) small, white
   haricot beans
2 medium-size potatoes
12 ounces (350 g) thin, green
   beans
12 ounces (350 g) zucchini
   (courgettes)
2 carrots
2 leeks
1 turnip
sea salt

freshly ground black pepper
4 ounces (120 g) small
   macaroni

FOR THE *PISTOU* SAUCE
2 ripe tomatoes
4 to 6 cloves of garlic
1 cup (120 g) of fresh basil
   leaves
1 cup (120 g) freshly grated
   Parmesan
6½ tablespoons (100 ml) olive
   oil
½ cup (60 g) grated Gruyère
   cheese, to serve

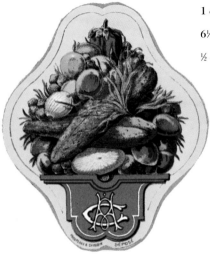

Soak the haricot beans for at least 6 hours. Drain, rinse, and drain again. Put in a saucepan, pour in 2¼ quarts (2 liters) cold water and bring to a boil. Skim if necessary.

Prepare the other vegetables. Peel and chop the potatoes; top and tail the beans, then cut into segments; slice the zucchini; scrape or peel the carrots; slice and wash the leeks; peel and chop the turnip. Ensure the pieces are no larger than 1½ inches (4 cm).

After 45 minutes add the vegetables to the pan, cover, and simmer for 45 minutes, or until tender. Season with salt and freshly ground black pepper. Add the macaroni and finish cooking the soup, uncovered.

Meanwhile, prepare the *pistou* sauce. Blanch, skin, seed, and chop the tomatoes. Using a large mortar and pestle, pound the garlic, then add the basil leaves and pound well. Work in the chopped tomatoes and half the Parmesan, then add the olive oil a little at a time, mixing it in as for a mayonnaise. Alternatively, combine everything in the food processor, taking care not to over-process the sauce. Stir 1 ladleful of the soup liquid into the sauce, then pour into the soup and leave to settle and infuse for a few minutes over a low heat. Combine the remaining Parmesan with the Gruyère and serve in a bowl at the same time as the soup.

Potage Saint-Germain
Fresh Pea Soup

A DELICATE PEA SOUP flavored with chervil. The Saint-Germain in question is the Comte de Saint-Germain, Louis XV's war minister, whose name blesses preparations involving peas. Reduce the amount of water to 1 cup (250 ml) in the recipe below, go easy on the blending, and, voilà, you have purée Saint-Germain, a good accompaniment to fish and veal.

	Serves 4	
2¼ pounds (1 kg) fresh, baby, garden peas, in the pod		4 tablespoons (60 ml) light cream
hearts of 3 lettuces	a few sprigs of parsley	sea salt
12 pearl onions	6 tablespoons (90 g) butter	freshly ground black pepper
several sprigs of chervil	1 small egg yolk	small croutons, to serve

SHELL THE PEAS, SHRED THE LETTUCE hearts, chop the onions, and snip the fresh herbs. In a large, heavy-bottomed saucepan, melt 4 tablespoons (60 g) butter, then add the vegetables and herbs, and cook gently for 5 minutes, stirring frequently.

Pour in 5 cups (1.2 liters) boiling water and simmer for 20 to 30 minutes, until the vegetables are very tender. Reserving 2 to 3 tablespoons of peas, transfer the vegetables and most of the liquid to a blender or food processor. Blend until smooth and return to the pan. Alternatively, push through a fine strainer, mashing the vegetables well with the back of a wooden spoon to extract as much pulp as possible. Whisk the liquid and purée until well combined.

Reheat gently. Combine the egg yolk and cream in a small bowl and stir in a little soup, then gradually add this liaison to the pan, stirring well. Season to taste with salt and freshly ground black pepper. Just before serving, stir in the reserved peas, whisk in the remaining butter, and add the croutons.

SOUPE AUX LENTILLES
Lentil Soup

LENTILS SEEM TO BE to the early 1990s what the kiwi fruit was to the previous decade—and after years of neglect, it is now a case of lentils with practically everything. As a lifelong loyal supporter of this legume, I am delighted to see them back in fashion. For me, no trip to France is complete without the purchase of at least one package of dark green, little *lentilles du Puy*. They cook quickly and cleanly, without disintegrating into an unappetizing mush, and they have a good strong flavor.

2½ cups (450 g) small, dark green lentils
2 tablespoons (30 ml) olive oil, plus extra for serving, if wished
2 tablespoons (30 g) butter, plus extra for serving, if wished

Serves 6

1 large onion
1 clove of garlic
1 large potato
1 carrot

1 thickly cut slice of smoked bacon, without the rind
1 bouquet garni
1 tablespoon (15 ml) tomato paste (purée)
sea salt
freshly ground black pepper

RINSE THE LENTILS WELL AND SOAK THEM for 10 minutes in cold water. Meanwhile, gently heat the oil and butter in a large, heavy-bottomed saucepan, and prepare the vegetables.

Chop the onion and garlic; peel and chop the potato; scrape or peel and then slice the carrot. Sauté the onion in the pan until browned, then add the drained lentils and the vegetables.

Chop up the bacon and add to the pan. Stir until everything is well mixed.

Add the bouquet garni and about 1½ quarts (1.5 liters) cold water to the pan. Bring gently to a boil and simmer for about 30 minutes, or until the lentils and vegetables are cooked and soft. Remove the bouquet garni. Reserving about 2 ladlefuls, blend the soup in a blender or food processor. Return to the pan, and stir in the reserved unblended mixture and the tomato paste. If the soup looks too thick, thin it down with a cup of boiling water.

Season to taste with salt and freshly ground black pepper. Serve piping hot. You might like to add a trickle of olive oil or a knob of butter to each bowl of soup.

Any leftover soup will keep very nicely in the refrigerator for a couple of days—just remember to add a little extra liquid when reheating.

GRATINÉE AU ROQUEFORT
Onion Soup with Roquefort

A CHEESE LOVER'S version of the celebrated soup. It is gutsy, simple, and effective–a good dish to
"delegate" to would-be helping hands, but make sure they don't burn the onions.
For a luxurious finishing touch, try spooning a little liaison of egg yolk and cream into each bowl, between
the top crust and the soup. Definitely not home fare as I remember it,
but recently enjoyed in a London restaurant.

Serves 4

1½ pounds (750 g) large, white
   onions
6 tablespoons (90 g) butter
2 teaspoons (10 g) flour
sea salt
freshly ground black pepper
a little nutmeg, grated or
   ground
2 to 3 tablespoons (30 to 45 ml)
   brandy
4 ounces (120 g) Roquefort
   cheese
8 to 12 thin slices French
   bread, lightly toasted
1 ounce (30 g) Gruyère cheese

SLICE THE ONIONS. IN A LARGE, HEAVY-bottomed saucepan, melt the butter and gently sauté the onion slices until soft, without letting them color. Sprinkle the flour over the onions and stir it in well. Pour in 5 cups (1.2 liters) boiling water and cook for 15 to 20 minutes. Heat the oven to 400°F. Season the soup with salt, freshly ground black pepper, a little nutmeg, and then the brandy.

Mash the Roquefort with a fork. Reserve 4 slices of French bread and spread the mashed Roquefort over the rest. Arrange the coated bread in individual ovenproof bowls, then pour in the soup.

Place a slice of the reserved bread on top of each serving, then grate the Gruyère over the tops.

Brown the toppings in the oven for about 10 minutes. Serve at once.

Potage à l'Oseille
Sorrel Soup

Fresh, green, and a little sharp, this is a lovely spring soup. Once the sorrel season is over, I use exactly the same method to make watercress or spinach soup.

1 pound (450 g) sorrel
2 tablespoons (30 g) butter
2 potatoes
1 egg yolk

Serves 4

6 tablespoons (90 ml) heavy
  cream
sea salt
freshly ground black pepper

Wash, trim, and roughly shred the sorrel leaves. In a large, heavy-bottomed saucepan, melt the butter. Add the sorrel leaves, and gently stew for a few minutes.

Peel the potatoes and cut into roughly 1-inch (2.5-cm) dice. Add to the sorrel, pour in 5 cups (1.2 liters) cold water, bring to a boil, and cook for 10 to 15 minutes more.

In a small bowl, combine the egg yolk and the cream, stirring in the cream gradually.

Transfer the soup mixture to a blender or food processor, reserving a few tablespoons of the liquid, and blend the soup.

Stir the reserved liquid into the egg and cream. Return the soup to the pan, then gradually add the egg and cream, whisking well. Season to taste, then reheat until very hot, but do not boil.

Potage Bonne Femme
Leek, Carrot, and Potato Soup

A simple and comforting soup. I have tried finishing it off with a dollop of *crème fraîche*, but have gone back to using butter, which somehow always tastes better with this combination of root vegetables.

2 waxy potatoes
3 large leeks
4 carrots
6 tablespoons (90 g) butter,
  plus extra for serving

Serves 4

a few sprigs of fresh thyme
2 bay leaves
1 or 2 cloves of garlic, peeled
sea salt
freshly ground black pepper

Peel the potatoes. Wash and trim the leeks, then scrape or peel the carrots. Chop the vegetables into roughly 1-inch (2.5-cm) cubes. In a heavy-bottomed saucepan, melt half the butter, then sauté the vegetables until lightly colored. Add the thyme, bay leaves, and garlic to the vegetables, then pour in about 5 cups (1.2 liters) boiling water. Simmer for about 30 minutes.

When the vegetables are cooked, blend the soup in the blender or food processor. Season to taste with salt and freshly ground black pepper. Serve piping hot, with a good knob of butter in each bowl.

SOUPE AU POIVRON ET À LA TOMATE
Roast Bell Pepper and Tomato Soup

BRIGHT RED, GUTSY, and fresh tasting. Serve chilled on a hot day.

Serves 4 to 6

3 red bell peppers
6 large ripe tomatoes
5 tablespoons (75 ml) fruity
  olive oil
3 cloves of garlic, halved

sea salt
freshly ground black pepper
1 teaspoon (5 g) sugar
leaves from a few sprigs of
  thyme and oregano, or

1 teaspoon (5 g) each of
  dried thyme and oregano
2½ cups (600 ml) chicken or
  vegetable stock
6–9 black olives
¼ baguette

HEAT THE OVEN TO 400°F. HALVE THE peppers and remove the seeds and white membranes. Halve the tomatoes and scoop out the seeds and excess pulp. Brush a roasting pan with half the olive oil, add the garlic cloves, reserving half a clove, and place the peppers on top of the garlic, cut sides down. Roast for about 10 minutes, then add the tomatoes, cut sides down. Season the tomatoes and sprinkle with the sugar, thyme, and oregano, reserving a few leaves. Roast for 15 minutes, until charred and bubbly. Leave to cool a little, then peel the peppers.

Whiz the peppers and tomatoes with their pan juices in a food processor and tip into a saucepan. Add the stock to the food processor, and whiz briefly, then add to the saucepan. Adjust the seasoning, and reheat over a low heat until piping hot. Alternatively, chill for at least 2 hours to serve cold.

Pit and chop the olives. Put in a cup, and sprinkle with the rest of the olive oil and herbs, mix and set aside or chill until needed.

Cut the bread into thin slices, rub with the cut side of the garlic, and toast under a hot broiler.

To serve, distribute the olive mixture between the croutons. Ladle the soup into suitable shallow bowls. Float a few olive croutons over each helping.

Vichyssoise aux Asperges et Fines Herbes

Asparagus and Herb Vichyssoise

Asparagus prices vary enormously—this is a soup I make as soon as the precious stalks have lost their early season novelty appeal, when their cost has come down to that of run-of-the-mill vegetables. This is not a difficult dish to make, but its texture and appearance will be much enhanced if you (a) conscientiously prepare the asparagus, removing all the strings (especially if you are using fat, white stalks), and (b) sweat the onions over a very low heat to prevent them from browning. Consume hot or chilled, depending on the weather. When I serve this vichyssoise chilled, these days I often finish it with thick plain yogurt rather than cream, but *yaourt* definitely did not feature in my original recipe.

the white parts of 4 large
  scallions (spring onions)
1 large potato
18 ounces (500 g) asparagus
3 tablespoons (45 g) butter
5 cups (1.2 liters) chicken
  stock (see page 12)
several sprigs each of tarragon
  and chives

Serves 4

a small bunch of parsley
sea salt
freshly ground black pepper
½ cup (120 ml) light cream (or
  a mixture of cream and
  yogurt, see above)

Prepare the vegetables. Peel and finely slice the scallions. Peel and chop the potato. Carefully trim the asparagus, discarding any tough woody ends and peeling off any knobby, stringy bits; cut and reserve the tips of 4 to 12 stalks (depending on size), then cut the remaining stalks into segments.

In a large, heavy-bottomed saucepan, melt the butter over a low heat. Add the sliced onions and sweat for a few minutes, stirring frequently and keeping the heat low so the onions do not color. Add the chopped potato and continue stirring for a few minutes, still over a low heat.

Add the asparagus segments to the onions and potato, pour in the stock, and gently bring to a simmer. Snip half the tarragon, chives, and parsley into the mixture and season lightly with salt and freshly ground black pepper. Now cover and simmer gently for about 20 minutes until the asparagus and

potato are soft. Add the reserved asparagus tips after about 15 minutes. Remove the asparagus tips from the pan and set aside after cooking. Leave the soup to cool for a few minutes, then purée. If the texture looks less than perfectly smooth, press the soup through a fine strainer. Check the seasoning.

If serving hot, pour the soup back into the pan, stir in the cream, and heat through gently. Snip the remaining herbs and stir them into the soup, then add the reserved asparagus tips at the last minute.

If serving chilled, stir in half the cream and 4 tablespoons of cold water—the soup tends to thicken as it gets cold. Leave the soup until cold and refrigerate for at least 2 hours, or until needed. Also chill the reserved asparagus tips. Just before serving, check the seasoning, snip in the remaining herbs, and stir. Swirl in the remaining cream and plop in a few ice cubes, then add the asparagus tips.

Soupe Fraîche aux Épinards et à l'Avocat

Chilled Spinach and Avocado Soup

WHENEVER I CAN find baby spinach and decent avocados in the market at the same time, usually for a month or so in the early summer–and sometimes again at the very end of that season–this soup features regularly on the menu. The nutty smoothness of the avocado combines well with the slightly peppery sharpness of the spinach.

1½ pounds (750 g) young tender spinach sea salt 3 ripe, blemish-free avocados 2 or 3 lemons	Serves 4	a few sprigs of flat-leaf parsley 2½ cups (600 ml) chilled chicken stock hot-pepper sauce, cayenne pepper, or harissa

DISCARD THE SPINACH STEMS AND ANY large ribs. Blanch in lightly salted boiling water for a couple of minutes; drain. Meanwhile, skin and chop the avocados. Transfer them to a blender or food processor, squeeze the lemons and add the juice, then the wilted spinach. Snip the parsley and add to the avocado and spinach mixture; blend until smooth. Add the stock and blend again.

Transfer to a large bowl. Season to taste with salt and a little hot-pepper sauce, cayenne pepper, or harissa.

Gradually whisk in about 2 cups (450 ml) water and perhaps a little extra lemon juice, until the soup has a nice consistency.

Refrigerate for at least 1 hour, or until needed. Adjust the seasoning.

Serve the soup with a couple of ice cubes in each bowl.

Velouté aux Champignons
Creamy Mushroom Soup

Observant readers will notice that this is one of the few times that I use chicken stock in a soup recipe instead of plain *château la pompe* (water from the faucet). The reason is that it makes a big difference to the flavor of the dish—one of those occasions when faking it with a stock cube just won't do.

Which type of mushroom to use? Any cultivated, very fresh mushrooms will give of their best in this recipe. At the moment I am favoring brown cap *champignons de Paris*. If you feel extravagant, follow a great *gourmand's* advice: Curnonsky concludes his splendidly creamy version of *potage aux champignons* with the observation that the soup "will obviously taste better with wild mushrooms."

Serves 4

1 pound (450 g) fresh mushrooms	3⅓ tablespoons (52 g) flour	6½ tablespoons (100 ml) heavy cream
½ lemon	5 cups (1.2 liters) chicken stock (see page 12)	sea salt
6 tablespoons (90 g) butter, plus extra to finish	1 or 2 egg yolks	freshly ground black pepper

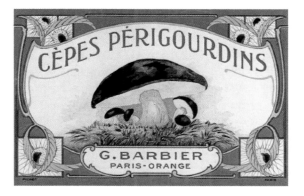

Wipe and trim the mushrooms. Keep aside 3 ounces (90 g), and very finely chop the rest. Finely grate the zest of the lemon, then squeeze the juice, reserving both. In a large, heavy-bottomed saucepan, make a roux. Melt 4 tablespoons (60 g) of the butter, stir in the flour, and cook gently for a couple of minutes, stirring constantly. Gradually pour in the chicken stock, a little at a time, stirring vigorously to prevent lumps forming, then add the chopped mushrooms and bring to a boil, still stirring. Reduce the heat and add the lemon juice and zest.

Cook gently for 20 to 25 minutes, stirring frequently.

Meanwhile, slice the reserved mushrooms very finely and sauté in the remaining butter. In a small bowl, combine the egg yolk or yolks with the cream. Stir in a ladleful of the soup liquid, then gradually pour the mixture into the pan, always stirring well; keep hot, but not boiling. Add the sautéed mushroom slices.

Season to taste with salt and a little freshly ground black pepper. Whisk in a good knob of butter and serve piping hot.

HORS D'ŒUVRE
Appetizers

NO FRENCH FAMILY lunch is complete without some little *hors d'œuvre*, or light first course, a clever appetizer that somehow simultaneously whets the appetite, yet takes the edge off it, while giving the cook a few extra minutes to organize the main dish. Most *hors d'œuvre* are as easy on the cook as they are appetizing: Many favorites need very little preparation indeed. What could be simpler to assemble than a few slices of *saucisson*, some black olives, and wedges of hard-boiled eggs? The dish welcomes you to the table without being in the least fussy.

My sister, Françoise, recently dampened my enthusiastic *hors d'œuvre* reminiscences by pointing out that the slices of *saucisson* were carefully counted and preprandial looting severely monitored. How could I forget . . . *saucissons*, expensive and, even in a less health-conscious decade, not known for their dietary qualities, never lasted long in our house. More often then not, the *saucisson* ration was accompanied by a substantial fresh salad. This varied subtly according to the people sitting around the table. It could be marinated mushrooms when a friend of our mother came to lunch, creamy cucumber for grandparents and older relatives, or celery root mayonnaise on the rare occasions our father managed to get away from the office. And if it was "just us," something like plain grated carrots or shredded cabbage would be the order of the day.

Salade d'Endive et de Poire au Roquefort

Endive and Pear Salad with Roquefort

I STILL REMEMBER THE first time I tasted the exciting combination of tender sweet pear, slightly bitter Belgian endive, and pungent Roquefort some years ago, in Brives in southwest France. I was mixing business and pleasure during a book fair. This salad works just as well before or after the main course.

6 heads of Belgian endive, red or white, rinsed and drained
2 ripe pears
a little lemon juice for brushing
3½ ounces (100 g) Roquefort cheese

Serves 4

FOR THE DRESSING
1½ tablespoons (22 ml) sunflower oil

1½ tablespoons (22 ml) walnut oil
2 teaspoons (10 ml) red wine vinegar
sea salt
freshly ground black pepper

SEPARATE THE ENDIVE LEAVES AND CHOP the large leaves. Halve and core the pears. Peel them if you like, brush with lemon juice, and slice thinly. Whisk the dressing ingredients together in a large, shallow bowl.

Toss the leaves in the dressing, then fold in the pear slices. Adjust the seasoning. Cut the Roquefort cheese into slivers, and don't worry if it crumbles a little.

Arrange the endive and pear slices on individual plates and place the Roquefort cheese on top. Season with extra pepper.

Rouille

Provençal Hot-Pepper Sauce

ROUILLE GETS ITS name from its attractive rust color, and its fieriness from small, red-hot peppers. With *tapenade* and *anchoïade* (see page 35), it makes an appetizing trilogy. Serve with an assortment of raw vegetables, steamed or boiled small new potatoes, or spread on warm toast.

2 small red chili peppers
1 small slice day-old white bread, crust removed
a little milk

Serves 4

2 cloves of garlic
1 egg yolk
sea salt

1 teaspoon (5 ml) tomato paste (purée)
6½ tablespoons (100 ml) olive oil
cayenne pepper, if wished

DISCARD THE STEMS AND SEEDS OF THE chilies (soak dried chilies in cold water first for a few hours). Soak the bread in a little milk, then squeeze to get rid of excess milk.

Using a blender, food processor, or mortar and pestle, combine the chilies, garlic, milky bread, egg yolk, salt, and tomato paste. Add the oil, a little at a time, until the mixture is very thick and smooth. Thin it out with a dash of cold water. Check the seasoning–if it's not hot enough for you, sprinkle a little cayenne pepper over the mixture.

POIREAUX VINAIGRETTE
Leek Salad

THE POOR MAN'S asparagus, the modest leek, really responds to being treated like its posh cousin. It is important to dress the leeks while they are still warm to let the flavors combine, and this appetizer is best eaten *tiède*–just above room temperature.

1½ pounds (750 g) fairly slim
   leeks
sea salt
a few sprigs of chives

Serves 4

FOR THE VINAIGRETTE
1 small hard-boiled egg
1 tablespoon (15 ml) Dijon
   mustard
sea salt
freshly ground black pepper
2 teaspoons (10 ml) white
   wine vinegar
about 6 tablespoons (90 ml)
   peanut oil

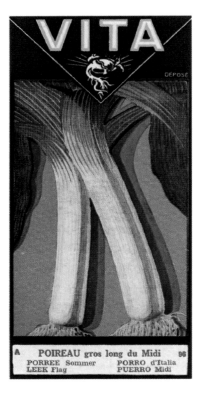

CUT OFF THE BEARDED ROOTS OF THE leeks and the tough end of the green tops. Slit the whole length of each leek with a sharp knife, and discard any discolored top layers. Gently open the leeks and rinse well under cold running water. Tie the leeks in bunches of 3 or 4 and cook in boiling salted water for 8 to 10 minutes. Transfer to a large strainer or colander and drain well.

While the leeks are cooking, prepare the vinaigrette. Grate the hard-boiled egg into a small bowl and mash with the mustard. Add a pinch of salt and a sprinkling of freshly ground black pepper, then stir in the vinegar and oil. Beat until well combined.

Gently squeeze the warm leeks with a very clean towel to remove excess moisture. Arrange the leeks on a dish like asparagus and pour the vinaigrette over them, then snip the chives and scatter them on top. Sprinkle a little extra pepper over the dish at the last minute and eat while still warm.

Salade de Poivrons à l'Avocat
Sweet Red Pepper and Avocado Salad

This colorful little appetizer has been a family favorite ever since avocados lost their *de luxe* dinner-party status and became staple fare for much of the year. Skinning peppers is a tedious task, so once I get going I always char more than I need for the salad; marinated peppers mature nicely in the refrigerator for a week or so. After a few days, you'll have a deep, piquant-sweet mixture that makes a good pasta sauce. Marinated peppers also do wonders for plain chicken pieces. Skin the chicken pieces, coat with the mixture, and season generously with black pepper. Bake gently for 30 to 45 minutes, in a 250°F oven, basting once.

Serves 4 to 6

3 ripe, unblemished red bell
   peppers
6 tablespoons (90 ml) good,
   strong-flavored olive oil
2 ripe avocados
1 lemon
sea salt
freshly ground black pepper
crusty bread, to serve

Wash and dry the peppers, then char them. I do that under the broiler, cursing quietly as I burn my fingers, turning the peppers until all the surfaces are charred and blistered. Leave them until cool enough to handle, then remove the skins–they will peel off easily if the peppers are charred enough. Don't worry about small stubborn patches of skin–the marinade will soften them.

Cut the peppers in half lengthwise and carefully remove the seeds, cores, and membranes. Slice into narrow strips and cut each strip into 2 or 3 segments. Put the peppers in a bowl, coat with the olive oil, cover with plastic wrap, and chill for at least 12 hours, during which time the mixture should be stirred once or twice.

Just before serving, halve the avocados, and remove the pits and skins. Cut into neat pieces or thin slices, squeeze the lemon, and moisten the avocados well with the juice. Combine with two-thirds of the marinated peppers and their juices, reserving the rest.

Season with a very little salt and more generously with black pepper. Serve with crusty fresh bread.

CHAMPIGNONS EN SALADE
Mushroom Salad

THIS LIGHTLY MARINATED salad makes a neat, fresh little appetizer and is a good way of making the most of not-very-exciting, cultivated mushrooms. It will keep well for a couple of days in the refrigerator.

12 ounces (350 g) fresh white button mushrooms 1½ lemons 4 tablespoons (60 ml) olive oil	Serves 4	sea salt freshly ground black pepper a few sprigs of fresh parsley

TRIM ANY SANDY STEMS OFF THE MUSH-rooms. Squeeze the lemons, then pour one-third of the juice into a bowl of cold water. Wash the mushrooms in the acidulated water. Dry them well with paper towels or a clean dishtowel, then slice them thinly straight into a salad bowl.

Stir in the remaining lemon juice, then trickle in the olive oil and stir until the mushroom slices are well coated. Season to taste with salt and freshly ground black pepper. Leave to stand in a cool place for a couple of hours. Before serving, finely chop the parsley and stir into the salad.

CONCOMBRES À LA CRÈME
Creamy Cucumber Salad

DEGORGING IS ONE of the great differences between French and Anglo-Saxon approaches. Generally speaking, the French always sprinkle cucumber flesh with salt, press it down with a weighted plate, and let it "sweat" its excess moisture and bitter juices for half an hour. The texture and flavor will be distinctly finer.

2 cucumbers coarse kosher salt a few sprigs of fresh tarragon	Serves 4	1 lemon ⅔ cup (150 ml) light cream freshly ground black pepper

WASH AND DRY (BUT DON'T PEEL) THE cucumbers. Run the prongs of a fork down the whole surface of each cucumber, then slice as thinly as you can, preferably with a mandolin or, alternatively, with a very sharp knife. Transfer the slices to a large strainer or colander and sprinkle with coarse salt. Place a plate or saucer on top of the cucumber slices and put a weight on it. Leave to stand for about 30 minutes.

Rinse the cucumbers thoroughly under cold running water. Pat dry with paper towels or a clean dishtowel. Transfer the cucumber slices to a bowl. Snip the tarragon leaves into the bowl. Squeeze the lemon, then pour in the juice and mix well. Gradually spoon in the cream, mixing it well into the salad. Season lightly with freshly ground black pepper, and refrigerate for at least 1 hour before serving.

CÉLERI RÉMOULADE
Celery Root Mayonnaise

A CREAMY-CRUNCHY traditional appetizer. *Sauce rémoulade* is a mayonnaise variation that is strong on mustard, and normally includes capers, gherkins, and sometimes anchovy. I am not alone in leaving the last three powerful ingredients out of this recipe, but they are great with cold cuts and potatoes.

Serves 4

1 to 2 celery roots (celeriac),
  about 1 pound (450 g) total
  weight
1 lemon
salt

FOR THE SAUCE *RÉMOULADE*
1 egg yolk
2 tablespoons (30 ml) strong
  Dijon mustard
1 teaspoon (5 ml) white wine
  vinegar
1 cup (250 ml) peanut oil
sea salt
freshly ground black pepper
a few sprigs of fresh parsley,
  tarragon, and chervil
paprika

PEEL AND GRATE THE CELERY ROOTS, then squeeze the juice of the lemon over them and blanch in boiling salted water for a few minutes. Drain well in a large strainer or colander, squeeze out the excess moisture with your hands, and leave to cool.

Meanwhile, prepare the sauce. Mix together in a bowl the egg yolk, mustard, and wine vinegar until well combined. Trickle in the oil, a few drops at a time to start, whisking vigorously until you have a thick mayonnaise—see page 13. Season with salt and freshly ground black pepper.

If the mayonnaise seems too solid, whisk in 1 tablespoon of boiling water. Finely snip the fresh herbs and stir into the sauce. Chill until ready to use.

Transfer the celery roots to a serving bowl and stir in the dressing, a spoonful at a time—the celery roots should be evenly coated. Leave to chill in the refrigerator for 1 hour at the very least, giving the salad an occasional stir.

Check the dressing before serving. Sprinkle with a little paprika and extra snipped herbs.

SALADE DE TOMATES
Tomato Salad

THIS IS THE simplest of appetizers, and one of the best, if–and that's a pretty hefty "if"–it is made with the right tomatoes. The right tomatoes are fragrant and firm-fleshed, juicy but not watery, and ripe but not mushy. The size doesn't matter all that much, but I am suspicious of many giants, particularly on supermarket shelves. Make a note of the recipe and save for a sunny day and the perfect tomatoes.

1 pound (450 g) "proper"
  tomatoes
2 shallots or ½ large white
  onion, if preferred
several sprigs of fresh parsley
  and chives or tarragon
4 tablespoons (60 ml) strong-
  flavored olive oil

Serves 4

2 teaspoons (10 ml) white wine
  vinegar
sea salt
freshly ground black pepper

TO SERVE
fresh bread
black olives

SLICE THE TOMATOES REASONABLY THIN and remove the core, seeds, and a little of the pulp. Arrange in concentric circles on a round platter, working toward the center.

Thinly slice the shallots or onion and scatter the rings or half-rings over the tomatoes. Snip the parsley and chives or tarragon and then scatter over the dish.

Whisk together the olive oil and vinegar, then season with sea salt and a little black pepper. Sprinkle the dressing over the salad as evenly as possible. Leave to stand for 15 minutes or so before you eat–it will taste infinitely better at room temperature. Mop up the juices with plenty of fresh bread and have a bowl of black olives on the table.

Tapenade
Black Olive Purée

A RELAXING APÉRITIF is the best prelude to an enjoyable meal. And no proper apéritif is complete without some homemade *amuse-gueule*, a tasty little "palate-tickler" that will keep everybody happy even if they have to wait for a late fellow-guest or a problematic dish. *Tapenade* served with croutons is a summer favorite, and much to be recommended with a glass of flinty cold Provence rosé, or pastis, if you prefer.

4 ounces (120 g) fleshy black
  olives, pitted
1 or 2 cloves of garlic
a little fresh thyme, summer
  savory, and cilantro leaf

Serves 4

strong-flavored olive oil
1 small anchovy fillet in oil
  (optional)
freshly ground black pepper

CHOP UP THE OLIVES AND CRUSH THE garlic. Discard the stems from the fresh herbs and shred the leaves. Pound together the olives, garlic, and herbs, using a mortar and pestle, gradually adding olive oil until you have a thick, smoothish paste.

Cut up and mash the anchovy fillet, if using, then work it into the paste, adding more olive oil. Taste and season with freshly ground black pepper. Alternatively, whizz all the ingredients together in the food processor–check the taste before seasoning.

Anchoïade
Anchovy Purée

ANCHOÏADE CAN BE served cold with crudités, or hot, spread over bread and toasted. There are many versions of this dish from Provence. My old favorite family recipe comes, I believe, from Draguignan.

8 ounces (225 g) salted
  anchovies, or 4 ounces
  (120 g) canned anchovy
  fillets in oil
2 to 4 cloves of garlic
1 tablespoon (15 ml) white
  wine vinegar

Serves 4

1 small hard-boiled egg
¼ large white onion
1 cup (250 ml) olive oil
thick slices of bread, to serve
freshly ground black pepper

IF YOU ARE USING SALTED ANCHOVIES, rinse them well under cold running water, then soak in fresh cold water for at least 1 hour, changing the water a couple of times. If using canned anchovies, drain off the oil.

Combine the anchovies with the garlic, vinegar, hard-boiled egg, and onion in the food processor, then gradually work in three-quarters of the olive oil. If you are not using a food processor, chop up the anchovies and garlic very finely, and combine with the vinegar. Chop up the egg and onion very finely, too, and stir into the anchovy mixture until well combined. Beat in the olive oil a little at a time.

Spread the anchovy purée over thick slices of bread. Sprinkle on the remaining olive oil and season liberally with black pepper. Pop under the broiler for a few minutes and serve hot.

Rillettes de Saumon
Salmon Rillettes

Traditional salmon rillettes are made with a mixture of cooked and smoked salmon. I prefer this version, which I often serve on buttered light rye bread with drinks before we sit down to the main course.

about 1 pound (450 g) good
   smoked salmon offcuts,
   trimmed and snipped into
   small pieces
tiny leaves from a few sprigs of
   thyme, or 1 teaspoon (5 g)
   dried thyme

Serves 6 to 8

juice and finely grated zest
   of 1 small unwaxed lemon
2 tablespoons (30 g) soft
   unsalted butter
3½ ounces (85 g) plain Boursin
   cheese

¼ teaspoon (1 g) paprika
cayenne pepper
freshly ground black pepper
sea salt
thinly sliced, buttered, light rye
   bread and a handful of
   watercress leaves, to serve

In a food processor, briefly whiz the pieces of smoked salmon with the thyme and lemon juice and zest. Scrape down the sides of the bowl, then add the butter and Boursin. Season lightly with the paprika, a touch of cayenne, and black pepper. Whiz again briefly until the mixture is combined, but still a little rough. Taste, and adjust the seasoning–salt, pepper or paprika. Chill for at least 20 minutes, longer if convenient. Remove from the refrigerator at least 10 minutes before serving.

Serve with or on slices of buttered rye bread, with a few watercress leaves.

Œufs Mimosa
Hard-Boiled Eggs with Anchovy Mayonnaise

A colorful appetizer that looks good on a buffet or party platter. Very retro!

4 extra-large eggs
6 tablespoons (90 ml) well-
   seasoned mayonnaise (see
   page 13)

Serves 4

a few sprigs of parsley
2 ripe tomatoes

1 romaine (cos) lettuce
2 teaspoons (10 ml) anchovy
   extract (essence)
2 anchovy fillets in oil
freshly ground black pepper

Boil the eggs for 10 minutes or so, then immerse in cold water until cool enough to shell. Meanwhile, prepare the mayonnaise (see page 13) and the other ingredients. Finely snip the parsley and slice the tomatoes, discarding the seeds and whitish cores–you'll need 8 slices. Tear out, rinse, and pat dry 8 to 10 presentable lettuce leaves.

Shell the hard-boiled eggs and halve them lengthwise. Carefully remove the yolks with a teaspoon; reserve 2 yolks. Mash the other yolks with the anchovy extract (use a fork), then combine with half the snipped parsley and the mayonnaise. Spoon the egg and mayonnaise into the halved egg white cases. Trim the bottom of any that look wobbly.

Arrange the lettuce leaves and tomato slices on a platter, then place a stuffed half-egg on each tomato slice. Cut each anchovy fillet into 2 strips, and place over each egg in a cross. Grate the reserved egg yolks over the dish–this is the mimosa effect. Sprinkle with the remaining parsley and a little black pepper. Refrigerate until ready to serve.

Melons Rafraîchis au Vin Doux
Chilled Melons with Sweet Wine

Just like pears and Camembert, melons are quite unpredictable. You can make sure you select a ripe melon by choosing a fruit with a good heavy feel to it. It should also give a little around the stem and at the opposite end. And if it is a Charentais or Cavaillon melon, it should also have a fruity fragrance. Infuriatingly, not every carefully chosen melon delivers. For informal meals, I always taste a silver of each melon and make sure every plate has a wedge of the day's glorious best and disappointed worst–no favoritism. For grander occasions, I go back to the old family special below. I have been delighted to notice that it seemed to be a popular summer dish in Anjou and Touraine restaurants–with the flesh carefully pressed into melon balls, of course, but that's definitely not a trick *maison*.

Serves 4

two 1-pound (450-g) promising
    Charentais or Cavaillon
    melons, or 4 smaller Ogen
    melons
½ bottle chilled sweet white
    wine, such as Coteaux du
    Layon, Vouvray doux, or
    Beaumes de Venise
freshly ground black pepper, if
    wished

Halve the melons and scoop out the seeds and any membranes. If you are using small Ogen melons, remove the stalk ends. Trim the bottoms if necessary so the melon "cups" stand upright. Refrigerate for at least 40 minutes.

To serve, pour a little chilled wine into each cup–the equivalent of a small glass. Float an ice cube or two on top and serve at once. For a special finishing touch, try it also with a little sprinkling of black pepper around the rim of each melon cup.

Macédoine de Légumes Frais à la Mayonnaise

Fresh Vegetable Medley with Mayonnaise

A SUBSTANTIAL APPETIZER, popular with people who prefer their vegetables cooked. Add hard-boiled eggs and leftover strips of meat, fish, and shellfish and you have *salade Russe*. Both dishes are pleasing when homemade, but best avoided in unknown commercial establishments. Canned *macédoine* is simply poor convenience food. I used to wonder what, if anything, Alexander the Great of Macedonia had to do with this particular dish. (Is he not linked with another dish, the early form of sorbet he fatally consumed during a long banquet after battle?) The answer was somewhat far-fetched. The *Petit Robert* dictionary, in a moment of levity, explains that *macédoine* is a light-hearted reference to the fact that Macedonia was once inhabited by a medley of people . . .

10 ounces (300 g) carrots
10 ounces (300 g) baby turnips
8 ounces (225 g) green beans
2⅔ cups (400 g) baby peas, or
   1½ cups (225 g) frozen *petits pois*
8 ounces (225 g) new potatoes
sea salt
½ lemon

Serves 4

1 tablespoon (15 ml) olive oil
freshly ground black pepper
⅔ cup (150 ml) mayonnaise
   thinned down with
   1 tablespoon (15 ml) water
a few sprigs of fresh parsley,
   tarragon, chives, and chervil

BRING A LARGE SAUCEPAN OF WATER TO a boil and start preparing the vegetables. Peel the carrots and baby turnips, then dice into small ¼-inch (0.5-cm) cubes. Top and tail the beans, then slice them into small ¼-inch (0.5-cm) segments; shell the peas; then scrape and dice the new potatoes.

Add 2 teaspoons of salt to the boiling water. Throw in the carrots and turnips and bring back to a boil. Add the beans, peas, and potatoes. If using frozen *petits pois*, don't add them until the water has come back to a boil the second time. Boil for 5 to 10 minutes more, or until all the vegetables are cooked, but not too soft. Drain well and transfer to a dish. Squeeze the lemon and sprinkle the juice and olive oil over the vegetables, then season lightly with a little salt and freshly ground black pepper.

Leave until completely cool, then gently stir in the mayonnaise and snip the fresh herbs over the dish. This dish will keep in the refrigerator for a day or two.

CHOU EN SALADE
Shredded Cabbage Salad

THIS WAS A FAVORITE salad appetizer when I was a schoolgirl, ravenous but worried about my weight. I used to wolf down platefuls of the blissful stuff. To this day I prefer it to more complex coleslaw variations. The secret lies in the shredding (long, thin strips of cabbage imbibe the vinaigrette dressing better than short, stubby pieces) and in the time spent marinating.

1 small white cabbage
1 tablespoon (15 ml) white
  wine vinegar

Serves 4

6 tablespoons (90 ml) peanut
  or olive oil
sea salt
freshly ground black pepper

DISCARD ANY BLEMISHED OUTER LEAVES. Cut the cabbage into 8 wedges and remove the core with a sharp knife. Rinse in cold water, shake well, and pat dry with paper towels or a clean towel. Using a sharp knife, carefully shred the cabbage into fine strips, discarding any large ribs. Alternatively, use the shredding disk of a food processor.

Transfer the shredded cabbage to a salad bowl and stir in the vinegar. Pour in the oil, stir to coat, and season to taste with salt and freshly ground black pepper. Chill for a couple of hours, giving the salad a good stir once or twice.

Check the taste of the dressing before serving and add a little salt, pepper, or oil as necessary. The salad tastes best when generously coated with a strong dressing.

CAROTTES RÂPÉES
Grated Carrot Salad

MY FAVORITE WAY to ingest this vitamin-laden vegetable. The sweetness of the carrots makes this salad very appealing to veg-resistant children. Best made with mature organic carrots.

14 ounces (400 g) carrots
1 lemon
1 hard-boiled egg
4 ounces (120 g) pitted black
  olives

Serves 4

5 tablespoons (75 ml) olive oil
sea salt
freshly ground black pepper
a few sprigs of fresh parlsey

PEEL AND GRATE EACH OF THE CARROTS. Transfer to a salad bowl. Squeeze the lemon, add the strained juice, and toss the carrots to coat well. Grate in the hard-boiled egg, then stir in the black olives. Add the olive oil, toss well, and season lightly with salt and freshly ground black pepper. Refrigerate for at least 1 hour. Remove from the refrigerator 20 minutes or so before serving. Check the seasoning and add a little extra oil, salt, or pepper if necessary. Snip and stir in the parsley at the last minute.

ENTRÉES CHAUDES
Hot Appetizers

LET ME BE FRANK about this. Several of the recipes in this section are at least as fiddly and time-consuming to prepare as main fish or meat courses. Don't let this put you off. There are a number of delectable, old-fashioned classics waiting to make a comeback in the next 20-odd pages, from *tarte à l'oignon* to *gougère, escargots au Riesling* to *crêpes farcies*.

The solution is to regard them rather as the French are doing–as first courses for special occasions or as *plats uniques*, low on fish and meat, but perfectly satisfying in every other respect, when things are more casual and meals one or two courses shorter.

I think of these *entrées chaudes* as hot (or warm) snacks, some grander than others, of course, but all very relaxed, *très sympathiques*, and maybe a little tentative. The French don't really have a word for snack. The nearest to it is *casse-croûte*, which means to break the crust. *Entrées chaudes* are more elaborate, but they do break the edge of your appetite. You tend to eat them while you are hungry. Perhaps this is why they are so enjoyable: the best dish may be yet to come, during this meal or some future, more structured occasion, but who cares just now.

CRÊPES FARCIES AUX ÉPINARDS
Crepes Stuffed with Spinach

BRING BACK OLD-FASHIONED savory crepes! They are fun to make, good-natured enough to keep overnight, and they take kindly to leftovers. The rather beery batter below was adapted *en famille* a long time ago from a totally beery Raymond Oliver recipe that had only a little milk to melt the butter in. Vary the blend to suit your taste–there are no hard-and-fast rules.

The ham, shallot, and mushroom mixture I suggested as a soufflé alternative (see page 47) also works well as a crepe filling. So does a little leftover cold chicken, briefly sautéed with snipped tarragon leaves, then stirred into the béchamel. Add a little heavy cream and leave out the Gruyère.

heaping 1¼ cups (175 g) flour
sea salt
3 eggs
4 tablespoons (60 g) butter,
  plus extra for the filling and
  to finish
about ¾ cup (175 ml) milk
about ¾ cup (175 ml) beer
oil for greasing
	Makes about 15 crepes	FOR THE FILLING
		4 cups (450 g) cooked and
		  drained spinach, or 3 pounds
		  (1.5 kg) fresh spinach
		1½ cups (350 ml) thick
		  béchamel (see page 13)
		4 ounces (120 g) Gruyère
		  cheese
		sea salt
		freshly ground black pepper
		grated nutmeg

SIFT THE FLOUR AND SALT INTO A BOWL and make a well. Beat the eggs as for an omelet and melt the butter with a little of the milk. Using a small whisk, gently stir together the flour and eggs, then gradually pour in the milk and beer. Stir lightly until the batter is smooth and just thick enough to coat your finger. Add the melted butter and stir a little longer. Strain through a fine strainer or *chinois* and preferably leave to stand for a couple of hours.

To cook the crepes, very lightly grease a smooth, heavy-bottomed skillet. I use a wad of paper towels dipped in a little oil. Heat the pan until very hot and ladle in just enough batter to cover the bottom thinly–tip the pan to spread it evenly. Cook over a medium-high heat until the underside is golden. Turn over with a spatula and cook the other side. The first crepe sometimes sticks a little, but it tends to become easier as it gets going. If your first crepe looks a little dry, whisk a little more melted butter into the batter; if it

is thin and tears easily, sift in a little flour and whisk in briskly. Re-grease the pan if necessary. Allow 2 to 3 minutes for each pancake. Once cooked, stack on a plate and cover with foil until ready to use. This is a good time to take a break: The crepes will keep overnight in the refrigerator.

Heat the oven to 400°F. Prepare the filling. If using fresh spinach, trim, rinse, and blanch in boiling water. Drain well in a colander, pressing hard to get rid of excess moisture; chop finely. Sweat the chopped spinach in a little butter. Stir into the béchamel. Grate the Gruyère and stir half into the spinach sauce. Season with a little salt, a generous amount of black pepper, and a good pinch of nutmeg.

Butter a baking dish. Spoon some filling over each crepe. Roll up and place in the dish. Sprinkle the crepes with the remaining Gruyère, dot with butter, and bake for 10 to 15 minutes, until hot and golden brown. Serve at once.

ŒUFS BROUILLÉS PLM
Scrambled Eggs PLM

THE FIRST DISH my father taught me to cook, and a perennial family treat. Sometimes this was pure comfort food to cheer ourselves up in a still-cold house after the drive from Paris. The cupboards may have been empty, but we never arrived without a dozen eggs, a salad, and some bread. Herbs were usually to be found in the garden–however puny–and the *beurre salé* kept well in the refrigerator from one visit to the next. When PLM (my father's initials) was in charge of the menu he often gave them to his guests as an appetizer, but the tradition has continued; when in doubt we have scrambled eggs for supper.

6 extra-large eggs at room
  temperature
sea salt
freshly ground black pepper
butter

Serves 2 or 3

sprigs of fresh herbs–tarragon,
  chives, parsley, or chervil, as
  liked
toast or crusty bread, to serve

IN A BOWL, WHISK 5 EGGS BRISKLY, BUT without letting them become fluffy. Season with salt and freshly ground black pepper. Melt a good knob of butter in a heavy-bottomed saucepan over a very gentle heat. Tilt the pan to coat its sides with butter.

Pour in the eggs and cook gently. Stir frequently with a wooden spoon and keep the heat very low–this is not a dish you can abandon to have a chat on the phone, but you can snip the fresh herbs finely while keeping an eye on the egg mixture. When the eggs begin to look set and cooked, add the remaining egg. Stir it in well, remove from the heat and add the snipped herbs with, if you like, a little extra butter.

Adjust the seasoning. Serve at once, with toast or crusty bread. Immerse the pan in very hot water immediately–this will save a lot of effort later.

ŒUFS GRATINÉS
Gratin of Eggs and Gruyère

A CREAMY, HOT egg appetizer that slips down a treat.

butter
5 ounces (150 g) Gruyère or
  strong sharp cheddar cheese
4 extra-large eggs

Serves 4

6 tablespoons (90 ml) heavy
  cream
sea salt
freshly ground black pepper

HEAT THE OVEN TO 325°F. GENEROUSLY butter a medium-size gratin dish or 4 small ovenproof ramekins. Grate the cheese, then spread a good layer over the bottom of the dish or dishes, reserving about one-third for the topping. Carefully break the eggs over the grated cheese.

Spoon 1 tablespoon of cream over each egg and season well with salt and freshly ground black pepper. Sprinkle the remaining grated cheese over the eggs with the remaining cream. Dot with butter and cook in the oven for about 15 minutes, until golden. Serve very hot.

ŒUFS BROUILLÉS À LA TOURANGELLE
Scrambled Eggs with Rillettes

RILLETTES ARE A SPECIALTY of Touraine. They are made from pieces of pork, or goose, slowly cooked in fat in a large cauldron until molten to a soft, fatty pâté–definitely a bit of an acquired taste, but detours are made by addicts of *rillettes* to find a *charcutier* who prepares them properly. They are a traditional local appetizer or snack, served with chunks of bread and a glass of cool Vouvray. Packed in little waxed pots, they will keep chilled for up to three weeks–well worth bringing back from France if you become addicted. They are particularly good combined with scrambled eggs. And so are salmon *rillettes*, a satisfying combination of fresh and smoked salmon, spices, lemon juice, and butter–not from Touraine, but now appearing on delicatessen counters everywhere.

3 ounces (90 g) *rillettes* of
  duck, pork, salmon, or tuna
6 extra-large eggs
freshly ground black pepper

Serves 2 or 3

1 tablespoon (15 ml) *crème
  fraîche*
a few sprigs of parsley
toast, to serve

MELT HALF THE *RILLETTES* IN A HEAVY-bottomed saucepan over a very low heat. Tilt the pan around until its sides are coated with fat.

In a bowl, whisk 5 of the eggs and season the mixture generously with freshly ground black pepper–the *rillettes* are fairly salty so there is no need to add salt.

Pour the eggs into the pan and cook patiently, keeping the heat low and stirring frequently with a wooden spoon, until they are almost set. Stir in the remaining egg and *rillettes*, then the *crème fraîche*. Remove from the heat. Snip a little parsley over the scrambled eggs and serve at once, with hot toast passed around separately.

ŒUFS EN MEURETTE
Eggs in Red Wine

THE BURGUNDIAN WAY of poaching eggs—in a strong red wine sauce. Keeping poached eggs warm is a little fiddly, so I have gone for the easier option of poaching the eggs at the last minute in simmering water with a few drops of vinegar, rather than in the red wine stock. Incidentally, the sauce is perfect with steak and monkfish.

Serves 4

4 extra-large eggs
4 slices French bread
red wine vinegar

FOR THE SAUCE
2 shallots
1 small onion
2 cloves of garlic
at least ½ bottle full-bodied red
    wine
1 sprig of thyme
1 bay leaf
1 sprig of parsley or chervil
6 tablespoons (90 g) butter,
    plus extra to finish the sauce
1 tablespoon (15 g) flour
sea salt
freshly ground black pepper

PREPARE THE SAUCE. PEEL AND HALVE the shallots, onion, and garlic, reserving half a clove. Make up the red wine to 3¼ cups (750 ml) with water. In a saucepan, bring the wine and water to a boil with the shallots, onion, garlic, thyme, bay leaf, and parsley or chervil. Boil until reduced by half.

Meanwhile, mash together 4 tablespoons (60 g) butter and the flour and divide the paste into 4 small pieces. Strain the hot wine stock through a strainer into a smaller saucepan and then gradually add the butter and flour paste, whisking in the pieces one by one. Whisking all the time, simmer the sauce for 2 minutes until it has thickened. Season to taste with salt and freshly ground black pepper; and then keep hot, stirring occasionally.

Rub the bread with the cut side of the remaining garlic and fry in butter until golden brown on both sides; keep warm.

Rinse out the first saucepan, pour in at least 7½ cups (1.8 liters) of boiling water, add a trickle of red wine vinegar, and bring back to a boil. Stir until the water swirls around, then lower the heat a little, and carefully poach the eggs for 1 to 2 minutes. I find it easiest to use a ladle to lower the eggs into the simmering water, and a draining spoon to lift them out. Drain the eggs well on an impeccably clean, folded towel; trim with scissors if they look too messy. Arrange one egg on each of the slices of fried bread. Whisk a few small knobs of butter into the sauce to make it look glossy, spoon it over the eggs, and serve.

OMELETTE AUX FINES HERBES
Herb Omelet

THIS IS ONE of the first recipes I remember watching someone cook, one of the first I wrote down, and, to my shame twenty years later, one that I still can't report to have constant success with.
My mentor, Madame Boucher, used to manage 16 eggs at the same time in an incredibly heavy, huge, battered black skillet.
Invariably her omelets turned out moistly creamy inside, packed with specks of fragrant herbs from the garden, and golden on the outside. Accompanied by the other deceptively simple dish, *pommes de terre sautées* (see page 124), another Boucher triumph, it made a perfect dinner.

several sprigs of fresh
  herbs–tarragon, or chives,
  and parsley, and/or chervil
4 extra-large eggs
1 tablespoon (15 ml) milk

Serves 2

sea salt
freshly ground black pepper
3 tablespoons (45 g) butter,
  plus a little extra to finish

SNIP THE HERBS VERY FINELY AND reserve. In a bowl, using a fork, beat the eggs briskly with 1 tablespoon of cold water and the milk for about 20 seconds. Whisk in half the snipped herbs and season to taste with salt and freshly ground black pepper.

Meanwhile, heat a smallish, heavy-bottomed skillet until very hot. Add 2 tablespoons (30 g) butter and swirl it around to coat the pan. Before the butter starts browning, pour in the beaten eggs. Reduce the heat a little. Cook the omelet, shaking the pan to prevent the eggs from sticking, and stirring the edges of the mixture toward the center of the pan when it begins to set.

As soon as the eggs are no longer liquid, but still looking moist, slip the rest of the butter under the omelet and sprinkle half the remaining herbs on top. Gently tilt the handle of the pan down toward you and fold the omelet back toward the center with the help of a metal spatula. Now lift up the handle of the pan away from you and turn the omelet upside down onto a heated plate. Trail a little extra butter over the omelet, sprinkle with the rest of the *fines herbes,* and serve.

PIPÉRADE
Tomato and Sweet Pepper Omelet

MY SUCCESS RATE with large folded omelets being more than erratic, I have long been a fan of *pipérade*, the celebrated sweet bell pepper and egg dish from the Basque country. It looks appetizing, requires no folding, and is a good dish to serve when you haven't got a great deal of time at the finish. Prepare the vegetable purée ahead and reheat it while you are whisking the eggs. Serve with Bayonne ham, bread, and a green salad for an easy supper or brunch.

1 large red bell pepper
1 onion
olive oil or bacon fat
3 cloves of garlic
3 or 4 ripe tomatoes
a pinch of dried thyme
1 bay leaf

Serves 4

2 slices Bayonne or similar
   cured ham
a little sweet vermouth or
   1 teaspoon (5 g) sugar
sea salt
freshly ground black pepper
8 extra-large eggs

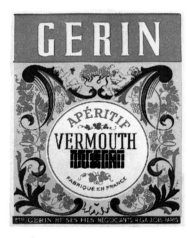

WASH AND DRY THE PEPPER, THEN CUT IT in half and remove the seeds, core, and membrane. Char under the broiler, uncut side up, until the skin is blistered. When the pepper is cool enough to handle, remove the skin and cut the flesh into small strips.

Chop the onion. In a large sauté pan or skillet, heat a little olive oil or bacon fat and cook the onion with the whole garlic cloves, keeping the heat low. Blanch the tomatoes, then remove the skins and seeds and chop up the flesh. Add with the pepper, thyme, and bay leaf to the onion and cook for about 15 minutes, stirring occasionally, until you have a thickish, chunky purée.

Chop the ham into pieces and add to the purée, with a sprinkling of sweet vermouth or 1 teaspoon of sugar to take away any

acidity. Season to taste with salt and freshly ground black pepper. Remove the garlic cloves and bay leaf. A few minutes before serving, reheat the pepper mixture.

Break 4 eggs into each of 2 bowls and beat briskly with a fork. Divide the pepper mixture between the 2 bowls and combine well with the beaten eggs. Grease 2 medium skillets with olive oil and heat both pans and the broiler. When the pans are hot, pour in the mixture and cook for a few minutes over a low heat, stirring frequently, until the bottom of the *pipérade* is set.

Finish off under the broiler for a couple of minutes, until lightly set and just colored. I find it easier to produce a moist *pipérade* using 2 small skillets, but you might prefer to cook it in a single batch. Serve at once.

SOUFFLÉ AU GRUYÈRE
Cheese Soufflé

NOT EXACTLY AN original dish, I know, but one that is hard to beat and never fails to bring pleasure to the palate.

Serves 4 to 6

1 cup (250 ml) milk
1 bay leaf
sea salt
freshly ground black pepper
6 tablespoons (90 g) butter,
  plus extra for greasing
½ cup (75 g) flour

5 eggs
1 teaspoon (5 g) strong Dijon
  mustard
grated nutmeg
4 ounces (120 g) Gruyère or
  other strong hard cheese

BRING THE MILK TO A BOIL WITH THE BAY leaf, a pinch of salt, and a little black pepper; take off the heat. Melt the butter, add the flour, and cook gently for a couple of minutes, stirring constantly with a whisk. Pour in the hot milk, whisking briskly and bring to a boil. Reduce the heat and simmer until the sauce is smooth and thick, stirring frequently; remove from the heat.

Separate the eggs, then whisk the yolks into the sauce. Season with a little salt and pepper, the mustard, and a pinch of nutmeg.

Grate in the Gruyère. The mixture can be set aside for a while at this stage.

Heat the oven to 375°F. Generously butter an 8-inch (20-cm) soufflé dish. Whisk the egg whites until stiff. Using a large metal spoon, gently fold a little whisked egg white into the sauce. Fold in the rest thoroughly, working lightly and upward, to keep in as much air as possible. Pour into the prepared soufflé dish, level with a spatula, and bake for 25 to 35 minutes, until brown and well risen. Serve at once.

ESCARGOTS AU RIESLING
Snails with Wine Sauce

A VERY GOOD way of serving snails if you don't happen to have the necessary equipment to extract them from their shells. You can, of course, start from scratch, with live snails, in which case this is a real plan-ahead recipe, as you have to starve them for a week before you start cooking. I know I am too feeble-hearted to last the course and likely to let the snails loose in the dead of night, so I use good-quality canned *escargots* in London and freshly cooked ones from the *charcuterie* in France.

If you are disappointed not to see a proper snail butter recipe at this stage, turn to *moules farcies* (page 63) or *champignons farcis* (page 130). I love *beurre d'escargot* best of all with mushrooms and second best with mussels, but somehow not with snails.

Serves 4

2 shallots
2 cloves of garlic
a small bunch of fresh parsley
4 tablespoons (60 g) butter,
    plus extra for the toast
24 to 30 snails, canned and
    drained, or freshly cooked
8 slices French bread
6½ tablespoons (100 ml) Alsace
    Riesling
2 teaspoons (10 g) flour
½ cup (120 ml) *crème fraîche*
sea salt
freshly ground black pepper

FINELY CHOP THE SHALLOTS, 1 CLOVE OF garlic, and the parsley. Melt the butter in a sauté pan. Add the chopped shallots and garlic and half the parsley. Stir for a few minutes over a gentle heat. Add the snails and sauté for 2 to 3 minutes, stirring occasionally.

Meanwhile, prepare the toast. Cut the remaining clove of garlic in half. Rub the bread with the cut sides of the garlic, then butter lightly. Heat the broiler.

Pour the wine into the snail mixture and bring to a simmer. Sprinkle the flour over the mixture, stir and cook for 5 to 10 minutes. Stir in the *crème fraîche* and heat through gently. Toast the bread under the broiler.

Season the snails generously with sea salt and freshly ground black pepper.

As a finishing touch, gently sprinkle the remaining parsley over the snails and serve at once with the hot toast.

Croûtes au Fromage
Hot Cheese Croustades

A DISH I WELL REMEMBER circulating with at parties in my role of eldest daughter and *jeune fille de la maison*. French country bread, *pain de campagne*, was what we used. Monsieur Poilâne's bread is ideal if you are lucky enough to be able to find it. Try serving with a mixed leaf salad as a change from the ubiquitous goat cheese appetizer.

6 slices mixed-grain bread, medium cut
4 tablespoons (60 g) butter
7 ounces (200 g) Gruyère or similar strongly flavored hard cheese

Serves 4

2 small eggs
2 tablespoons (30 ml) *crème fraîche* or sour cream
grated nutmeg
freshly ground black pepper
a few sprigs of chives

HEAT THE BROILER. IF YOU PREFER, REMOVE the crusts from the bread. Butter on one side. The slices can be left whole, halved, or quartered–the smaller the better if you are serving them as finger food. Grate the cheese into a bowl and mix with the eggs and *crème fraîche*. Season to taste with nutmeg and

freshly ground black pepper. Generously spread the cheese mixture over the bread. Arrange in a flameproof dish and broil for a few minutes until golden brown.

Meanwhile, finely snip the chives. Serve hot or *tiède*, sprinkled with snipped chives and a little extra black pepper.

Croque-Monsieur Maison
Toasted Cheese and Ham

WHEN IN DOUBT, when you can't face the thought of cooking and can't think of anything to cook anyway, give them a *croque-monsieur*. Always in great demand from junior members of the family and not exactly frowned on by their seniors, the archetypal French café snack is wonderful emergency food.

3 tablespoons (45 ml) olive oil
8 slices of bread
4 to 6 tablespoons (60 to 90 g) butter

Serves 4

4 ounces (120 g) Gruyère or cheddar cheese

4 thick slices good cooked ham off the bone
2 to 3 teaspoons (10 to 15 ml) Dijon mustard
a few sprigs of chives

HEAT THE BROILER. IN A LARGE SKILLET, heat the olive oil and brown one side of each slice of bread. Remove from the pan, and butter the uncooked sides. Grate the cheese and spread over 4 slices, on the buttered sides. Heat under the broiler until melting.

Divide the ham between the remaining buttered pieces of bread, if necessary,

trimming the ham slices to fit. Spread some mustard over the ham. Snip the chives and sprinkle them over the ham.

Melt the remaining butter in the skillet. Heat the ham-covered slices of bread in the hot butter, fried sides down. Sandwich with the toasted cheese slices, cheese side down. Press well together and eat them very hot.

Feuilleté au Roquefort
Roquefort Cheese Puff

A MORE PROPER name for this recipe would be *demi-feuilleté au Roquefort*, since the pastry is very much a shortcut on traditional puff. The filling is rich and festive.

FOR THE PASTRY

1½ cups (225 g) flour
pinch of salt
6 tablespoons (90 ml) heavy
  cream
8 tablespoons (120 g) butter,
  plus extra for greasing
1 egg yolk and a little milk, for
  glazing

Serves 6 to 8

FOR THE FILLING

4 eggs
5 ounces (150 g) Roquefort
  cheese
6 tablespoons (90 g) cream
  cheese
6 tablespoons (90 ml) light
  cream
freshly ground black pepper
a small bunch of fresh chives

TO MAKE THE PASTRY DOUGH BY HAND, sift the flour and salt into a bowl. Make a well and add the cream. Lightly work the flour into the cream, adding a couple of tablespoons of very cold water if the flour isn't completely absorbed. Cut the butter into small pieces, add half to the flour and knead gently until absorbed, working the dough as little as possible. Divide the dough into 4 pieces, mix a bit of butter into each piece, then roll together to form a large ball.

If you are using a food processor, cut the butter into very small pieces. Briefly process the flour and salt. Add half the butter and process until the mixture resembles bread-crumbs. With the machine still running, add the cream and 1 tablespoon of cold water until the dough starts to form a ball and comes off the sides of the bowl. Add the remaining butter, dotting over the dough, and process just enough to mix it well in.

Whichever method you have used, once you have a ball of dough, turn it out onto a floured board, then flatten lightly with a floured rolling pin and fold and roll a couple of times. Chill the folded pastry for at least 30 minutes (but no longer than 1 hour, otherwise it hardens too much) before using.

Meanwhile, prepare the filling. Whisk the 4 eggs. In another bowl, mash the Roquefort with a fork. Combine the Roquefort, cream cheese, and cream, whisking the mixture until fairly smooth. Add the eggs and whisk well. Season generously with freshly ground black pepper and snip in the chives.

Heat the oven to 375°F. Separate the dough into 2 pieces, with one "half" slightly larger than the other. Roll out into circles. Grease a large, flat pan and spread the smaller dough circle on it. Prick well with a fork. Spoon the filling over the dough.

Cover with the remaining dough. Insert a pastry funnel in the center to allow the steam to escape. Seal the edges by lightly pressing together with dampened fingers. Score the top in a diamond pattern with a knife. Glaze the pastry with beaten egg yolk and a little milk. Bake for 40 to 45 minutes.

GOUGÈRE
Cheese Choux Ring

As SATISFYING TO make as to eat, particularly with a good glass of wine. This recipe is for a *gougère* ring. To make individual puffs, keep the paste balls at least 1 inch (2.5 cm) apart when you pipe or spoon them onto the baking sheet.

8 tablespoons (120 g) butter, plus extra for greasing 1 cup (150 g) flour 1 cup (250 ml) water salt	Serves 6	3 or 4 eggs 4 ounces (120 g) Swiss, Comté, or sharp farmhouse cheddar freshly ground black pepper dash of milk, for glazing

CUT THE BUTTER INTO DICE. SIFT THE flour onto a sheet of wax paper. In a heavy-bottomed saucepan, bring the water, diced butter, and a pinch of salt to a boil. The minute the liquid begins to boil, remove the pan from the heat. Quickly and all at once add the flour and immediately start stirring it in with a spatula or wooden spoon. Return to the heat and continue to stir briskly until the paste leaves the sides of the pan and looks smooth and a little shiny.

Remove from the heat and stir for 1 minute. Add the eggs, one at a time, mixing them in vigorously until the paste comes together again. Beat the last egg before you add it in, since you may need only a fraction of it: You should end up with a glossy, floppy paste, not a runny, liquid one. Continue beating for another minute or so

to give the paste more body. Cut the cheese into slivers and beat into the paste. Season with freshly ground black pepper.

Heat the oven to 375°F. Grease a baking sheet. Fit a pastry bag with a plain ½-inch (1-cm) tip and spoon the paste into the bag. Pipe a large ring of small balls of paste on the baking sheet, keeping them no farther than ¾ inch (2 cm) apart. If you don't like using a piping bag, you can use a tablespoon–the final effect will not be quite so tidy, but no matter. Brush the paste lightly with any remaining egg yolk mixed with a splash of milk.

Bake for about 30 minutes, until well risen and golden. Turn the oven off (and open the door if electric). Leave the *gougère* to stand for 5 minutes before taking it out. Serve hot or warm.

Petites Bouchées
Savory Puffs

A *BOUCHÉE* IS A MOUTHFUL, and I have always thought of these soft-centered little morsels as excellent "mouth-fillers." They certainly give the hostess or host time to control the subject of the conversation while guests are palatably occupied.

If you are getting out your pastry bag to make neat choux puffs, try piping some of the paste into small éclairs for contrast. These *bouchées* are good cold, but don't assemble them more than 1 to 2 hours ahead. Unfilled baked puffs or éclairs will freeze well, otherwise use them on the day you make them.

FOR THE CHOUX PUFFS
8 tablespoons (120 g) butter, plus extra for greasing
1 cup (150 g) flour
1 cup (250 ml) water
salt
3 or 4 eggs
freshly ground black pepper
1¼ cups (300 ml) thick béchamel (see page 13)

FOR THE SHRIMP FILLING
3 ounces (90 g) small cooked shelled shrimp
2 tablespoons (30 ml) heavy cream
cayenne pepper
a few sprigs of chives

Serves 6

FOR THE MUSHROOM FILLING
2 tablespoons (30 g) butter
6 ounces (175 g) cremini (brown cap) mushrooms
1 clove of garlic
2 teaspoons (10 ml) tomato paste (purée)
a few sprigs of parsley

FOR THE BLUE CHEESE FILLING
3 ounces (90 g) Fourme d'Ambert or similar blue cheese
1 stick of celery
2 tablespoons (30 ml) heavy cream
paprika

HEAT THE OVEN TO 375°F. MAKE THE choux pastry dough (see page 51) and pipe or spoon onto a greased baking sheet, keeping the paste balls at least 1 inch (2.5 cm) apart. Bake for about 30 minutes, until well risen and golden; leave to cool.

Meanwhile, prepare the fillings. To make the shrimp filling, press the shrimp dry between 2 sheets of paper towels, then cut in half. In a bowl, mix together one-third of the béchamel, the chopped shrimp, and the cream. Season with a good pinch of cayenne and a little salt. Snip in the chives.

To make the mushroom filling, melt the butter in a small skillet. Finely chop the mushrooms and garlic, then sauté over a medium heat. In a bowl, combine one-third of the béchamel with the tomato paste. Stir in the sautéed mushrooms and snip in the parsley. Season with salt and black pepper.

For the blue cheese filling, mash the cheese with a fork. Finely chop the celery. Mix with the remaining béchamel and the cream. Season with a good pinch of paprika.

Slit the puffs with a knife. Spoon the shrimp filling into one-third of the puffs, then the mushroom filling into another third, and the blue cheese filling into the rest.

TARTE À L'OIGNON
Onion Tart

A VERY ONIONY onion tart. The evaporated milk adds a distinctive rich sweetness to the filling. If you like a touch of *lardons* with onions, add about 3 ounces (90 g) chopped and sautéed smoked bacon drained on paper towels to the filling.

FOR THE TART CRUST
10 tablespoons (150 g) cold butter, plus extra for greasing
1½ cups (225 g) flour
pinch of salt
1 teaspoon (5 g) sugar
1 egg
1 egg white

Serves 8

FOR THE FILLING
2½ pounds (1.2 kg) large white onions
2 or 3 fresh sage leaves
4 to 5 tablespoons (60 to 75 ml) olive oil

3 eggs
6½ tablespoons (100 ml) evaporated milk or light cream
1 ounce (30 g) strong Gruyère or similar cheese
sea salt
freshly ground black pepper
grated nutmeg

PREPARE THE TART CRUST. CUT THE butter into small pieces. If you are using a food processor, combine the flour, salt, and sugar, then add the butter and process until the mixture looks like breadcrumbs. Add the egg and 5 or 6 tablespoons of cold water. Process until the mixture comes off the sides of the bowl. Remove the dough from the bowl, work lightly with your hands into a ball, and chill for at least 30 minutes.

Alternatively, cut up the butter and leave to soften. Sift the flour into a bowl with the salt and sugar. Make a well, add the butter, the egg, and 5 or 6 tablespoons of cold water. Mix with your fingertips without trying to get a smooth paste. Add a little more water if necessary–the paste should be supple but not soft. Form into a ball and chill as above.

Butter a large, loose-bottomed tart pan. Roll out the dough, then spread it into the greased pan, using your hands to press it in lightly without stretching it. Prick with a fork and chill for 10 minutes.

Heat the oven to 400°F. Line the dough with wax paper or foil and evenly fill with dried beans. Then bake the crust for 15 to 20 minutes.

Meanwhile, prepare the filling. Very thinly slice the onions–it doesn't matter if the slices break. Finely snip the sage leaves. In a large skillet, heat the olive oil, then gently sweat the onion slices with the chopped sage until soft and blond, but not too brown; keep the heat very low and the pan covered, occasionally lifting the lid to stir the onions. Allow a good 30 minutes for the onions to be really soft.

Remove the dried beans and lining paper from the pastry case. If the bottom still feels very soft, return the pan to the oven for a few minutes. Leave to cool a little, then brush the pastry with a little egg white. Turn the oven down to 375°F.

Lightly whisk together the eggs and the evaporated milk or cream. Stir into the onion mixture. Grate in the cheese. Season generously with salt and freshly ground black pepper and a little nutmeg. Pour into the prepared pastry shell and bake for 15 to 20 minutes. Serve warm rather than hot.

PISSALADIÈRE
Provençal Onion and Anchovy Tart

A FAVORITE SUMMER dish, and one that I have always thought of as "convenience" food, because we always used fresh bread dough from the village baker for the crust. Had I been more romantic I would perhaps have been reminded of the days of communal baking.

Now that I cannot easily get hold of fresh bread dough I use store-bought puff pastry dough, preferably fresh, and concentrate on gently cooking the filling until the onions sweetly melt. The tomatoes do not feature in original Provençal recipes for *pissaladière*, but I like their texture.

	Serves 6 to 8	
1 pound (450 g) store-bought puff pastry dough		2 tomatoes
butter or oil for greasing		a few sprigs of fresh thyme
1 small egg, separated		sea salt
		freshly ground black pepper
		1 teaspoon (5 g) sugar
FOR THE FILLING		about 24 canned anchovy fillets
2¼ pounds (1 kg) large white onions	4 tablespoons (60 ml) strong-flavored olive oil	about 12 black olives

PREPARE THE FILLING. THINLY SLICE THE onions. Heat the oil in a large skillet and sauté the onions over a very low heat. Meanwhile, blanch, peel, seed, and chop the tomatoes. Add the sprigs of thyme to the onions and continue to sauté over a low heat for 30 minutes, until the onions are very soft. Stir occasionally and be careful that the onions don't brown.

Heat the oven to 425°F. Roll out the dough to about ¼ inch (0.5 cm) thick. Grease a baking sheet. Cut the dough into a 10-inch (25-cm) square and spread it onto the sheet.

Cut the remaining dough into 4 strips, 10 inches (25 cm) long and ½ inch (1 cm) wide. Brush the surface of each strip with egg white, then stick one strip along each side of the dough square, brushed surface down.

Remove the sprigs of thyme from the skillet. Season the onion and tomato filling very lightly with salt and pepper and stir in the sugar. Spoon the filling evenly over the dough, keeping clear of the edges. Drain the anchovy fillets. Arrange attractively over the filling and dot about the black olives.

Beat the remaining egg white with the yolk and brush the edges of the dough. Bake for 15 to 20 minutes, then lower the heat to 375°F and bake for 5 to 10 minutes more, until the top is golden and the crust baked–check by lifting it a little with a spatula. Eat *tiède* or at room temperature.

QUICHE LORRAINE
Quiche Lorraine

CLOSE YOUR EYES and think of ten classic French dishes. I would be surprised if *quiche lorraine* did not feature somewhere on your list. You may be surprised to hear that this most famous French dish, the matriarch of the egg-and-cream filled family of tarts, derives its name from that very German word for cake–*kuchen*. The original *quiche lorraine* recipes from Nancy did not include cheese, but many people prefer it with, so I have added it as an optional extra. More important than the presence, or absence, of cheese is the quality of the bacon you use. The best bet (and a bit of a tall order) is traditionally cured, lightly smoked bacon, cut into very thick slices.

	Serves 6 to 8	
2 sticks (225 g) cold butter, plus extra for greasing		3 extra-large eggs
2½ cups (375 g) flour		⅔ cup (150 ml) cup heavy cream or *crème fraîche*
pinch of salt		freshly ground black pepper
		sea salt, if you like
FOR THE FILLING		2 tablespoons (30 g) butter
8 ounces (225 g) smoked bacon, cut into very thick slices	1 to 2 tablespoons (15 to 30 ml) olive oil	1½ ounces (45 g) Gruyère cheese (optional)

PREPARE THE TART CRUST. CUT THE butter into small cubes. If you are using a food processor, quickly whizz together the flour and salt. Add half the butter and process until the mixture looks like bread-crumbs. With the machine still running, add 5 or 6 tablespoons of cold water through the feed tube and process until the mixture forms a ball and comes off the sides of the bowl. Divide the ball into 4 pieces, return to the processor and add the remaining butter (dotted evenly over the dough). Process until well mixed.

Remove the dough from the bowl. On a floured board, roll it into a long rectangle (don't be too pedantic about this–rounded corners are fine), and then fold both ends toward the center. Roll out again and repeat 3 times. Chill for at least 30 minutes.

Alternatively, sift the flour and salt into a bowl. Make a well, add 5 or 6 tablespoons of very cold water, and lightly gather the flour into the water. Work the dough with your fingertips, then flatten it on a floured board.

Dot with the cubes of cold butter, press them in well, and fold over 3 times crosswise, like a letter, then fold 3 times lengthwise. Chill for 10 minutes and then roll and fold as above 3 more times, leaving the dough to rest in the refrigerator in between the rollings.

Heat the oven to 375°F. Butter a large, loose-bottomed tart pan. Roll out the dough, then spread it into the greased pan. Leave it to overhang a little from the pan; prick all over with a fork.

Line the dough with foil or wax paper and fill with dried beans. Bake for 15 minutes, then remove the beans and lining paper.

To make the filling, remove the rind from the bacon, if necessary, then cut into ¼-inch (0.75-cm) pieces. If you suspect that the bacon is very salty, blanch it in boiling water and pat it dry with paper towels. Heat the oil and sauté the bacon until golden; drain on paper towels. Spread the bacon evenly over the dough and press it in a little.

Beat the eggs and the cream, season with freshly ground black pepper. Pour into the pastry shell and dot with butter. If you are using Gruyère, grate it and sprinkle over the tart before adding the butter. Bake for 15 to 20 minutes, until set. Cover the tart with wax paper if it is coloring too quickly. Serve warm.

TARTE À LA MOUTARDE
Mustard Tart

A ROBUST TART for mustard lovers.

1 tart crust, half-baked (see *tarte à l'oignon* on page 53)	Serves 6 to 8	2 tablespoons (30 ml) light cream or evaporated milk
		3 tomatoes
FOR THE FILLING		sea salt
5 ounces (150 g) Gruyère or similar strong cheese		freshly ground black pepper
		dried thyme and savory
2 tablespoons (30 ml) strong Dijon mustard		2 tablespoons (30 ml) strong-flavored olive oil

PREPARE AND BAKE THE PASTRY SHELL. Heat the oven to 375°F. Make the filling. Grate the cheese and sprinkle one-quarter of it over the pastry. Mix the mustard with the cream or evaporated milk and pour over the grated cheese.

Blanch and peel the tomatoes. Cut into thin slices and remove the seeds. Sprinkle another quarter of the cheese over the mustard and cream mixture. Arrange the tomato slices on top. Season lightly with salt and pepper. Crumble in a pinch or two of dried herbs and cover with the remaining cheese. Sprinkle with the olive oil and black pepper, if desired.

Bake for about 20 minutes, until golden brown. Leave to cool slightly before serving to eat *tiède*.

TARTE À LA RATATOUILLE
Mixed Vegetable Tart

A MOST DEPENDABLE COMBINATION and a civilized way of using leftover *ratatouille* (see the recipe on page 121). If you are starting from scratch, however, halve the quantities given in the recipe and leave out the parsley and final tablespoon of olive oil. Serve, like other savory tarts, as an appetizer (for 6 to 8) or with a salad as a relaxed main course (for 4 to 6).

1 tart crust, fully baked (see page 53)	Serves 6 to 8	cooked ratatouille (see above)
		1 or 2 ripe tomatoes

PREPARE AND BAKE THE TART CRUST. Heat the oven to 375°F.

Chop and seed the tomatoes, then stir them into the ratatouille. Spoon the mixture into the prepared tart shell and smooth flat. Bake the tart for 10 to 15 minutes, then remove from the oven and leave to cool until barely warm before serving.

TARTE AUX EPINARDS
Spinach Tart

LIKE MANY OF its fellow savory tarts, *tarte aux épinards* is a very easy dinner-party first course, as it is best eaten barely warm and can be dealt with before the guests arrive. It would be dishonest of me not to mention that I sometimes make this dish with 1 pound (450 g) frozen spinach, well drained, instead of the fresh stuff when speed is of the essence—or the market spinachless.

1 tart crust, half-baked
   (see *tarte à l'oignon* recipe on
   page 53)

FOR THE FILLING
3 pounds (1.5 kg) fresh spinach
sea salt
5 tablespoons (75 g) butter

Serves 6 to 8

1 tablespoon (15 g) flour
1 cup (250 ml) *crème fraîche*
freshly ground black pepper
4 eggs
grated nutmeg
1 ounce (30 g) Gruyère or
   similar strong cheese

PREPARE AND BAKE THE TART CRUST. Make the filling while the tart shell is in the oven. Trim and wash the spinach. Wilt the leaves for 1 minute in a little salted boiling water. Drain well in a colander, pushing with a wooden spoon to extract as much moisture as possible; chop roughly. Melt a knob of butter in a pan, add the chopped spinach, and sweat for 1 minute; reserve.

In a saucepan, melt the remaining butter. Add the flour and cook for 2 minutes, stirring constantly. Spoon in the *crème fraîche* and cook until thickened, stirring frequently.

Season generously with salt and freshly ground black pepper; remove from the heat.

Beat the eggs thoroughly, then whisk them into the cream sauce. Fold three-quarters of this mixture into the spinach. Check the seasoning and add a little nutmeg. Pour into the half-baked tart shell. Top with the remaining cream and egg sauce. Grate the cheese and sprinkle over the tart.

Bake the tart at 375°F for about 20 minutes, until firm and golden. Leave to cool before serving—this tart tastes better *tiède* than hot.

Tarte aux Tomates Toute Simple
Tomato Tart

The best tomato tart I have ever eaten was in a Paris restaurant called Chez Francis near the Pont de l'Alma. The restaurant was all weathered mirrors and red banquettes, the clientele smooth and *très parisienne*. The tomato tart was a glorious concoction of melting tomatoes and buttery puff pastry. We have all had so much tomato doused in extra-virgin olive oil that I feel like campaigning for tomatoes anointed with butter. It brings out their sweetness. This recipe makes a perfect lunch for 4 people with a green salad, or a nifty dinner party appetizer for 6.

Serves 4 to 6

½ pound (225 g) store-bought chilled puff pastry dough in a sheet
1 ounce (30 g) butter
about 2¼ pounds (1 kg) ripe fresh tomatoes
2 tablespoons (30 ml) sunflower or mild-tasting olive oil

1 teaspoon (5 g) superfine sugar
1 level tablespoon (15 g) freshly grated Parmesan or Gruyère cheese

1 teaspoon (5 g) dried marjoram or oregano
a few leaves fresh basil, to finish
sea salt and freshly ground black pepper

Roll out the sheet of pastry dough. Generously butter the bottom and sides of a large, loose-bottomed tart pan. Place the dough in the pan, fit in loosely, then use a small, sharp knife to nick in crosses, and chill for at least 20 minutes.

Cut the tomatoes into thick slices (about ¼ inch/0.5 cm). Place on a clean towel or a double layer of paper towels. Sprinkle with salt and set aside for 15 minutes.

Heat the oil in a large skillet over a moderate heat. Sauté the tomatoes, sprinkled with sugar, in single layers, for 5 minutes each side. Reserve in a colander, and put a plate under it to collect the juices.

Heat the oven with a large baking sheet inside to 425°F. Take the dough out of the refrigerator, and sprinkle with the grated Parmesan and herbs. Arrange the tomatoes on top in overlapping circles, starting from the outside. Season again lightly, and sprinkle with 1 tablespoon of the tomato juices (the rest can be added to a sauce, soup, or dressing). Dot with the reserved butter and bake for 10 to 12 minutes, until golden and bubbling. Check that the pastry is baked through after 10 minutes: If the tomatoes are browning too fast, cover loosely with lightly crushed foil.

Serve warm rather than hot, decorated with torn basil leaves.

Jambon à la Crème
Ham in Cream and Port Wine Sauce

When I moved into my first flat after leaving university, my aunt Yvonée–who was a nice combination of intellectual, *gourmande,* and good cook–empathized with my situation. What could a novice cook and fledgling career girl impress her friends with? She gave me as a culinary bible her own copy of Curnonsky. She looked through her cards, books, and scrapbooks and went to a great deal of trouble to write down her chosen recipes. I was quite overwhelmed, but this quick-and-easy appetizer soon caught my eye.
It works well, followed by a large *salade niçoise,* as a quick supper–particularly if your guests turn up the minute you walk in.

Serves 4

4 thick slices of good cooked
  ham off the bone
2 tablespoons (30 g) butter
mini croissants, to serve

FOR THE SAUCE
6 tablespoons (90 ml) port wine
6 tablespoons (90 ml) tomato
  coulis (see page 15)

6 tablespoons (90 ml) sour
  cream or *crème fraîche*
sea salt
freshly ground black pepper

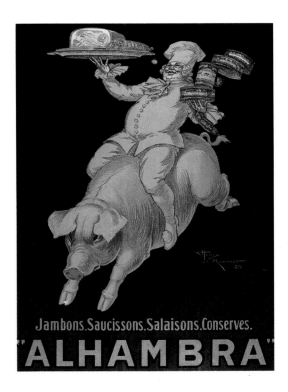

Jambons.Saucissons.Salaisons.Conserves.
"ALHAMBRA"

Heat the oven to 200°F. Heat the croissants and the serving dish. In a saucepan, combine the port wine, tomato coulis, and cream. Heat this mixture until very hot, but be careful not to boil, stirring frequently.

Meanwhile, melt the butter in a skillet and heat the ham. Roll each slice and place in the heated serving dish. Season the sauce with salt and plenty of ground black pepper. Pour over the ham and serve with the croissants.

POISSONS ET FRUITS DE MER
Fish and Seafood

OUR LOCAL PARIS STREET MARKET, rue Poncelet in the XVIIth, wasn't particularly distinguished by Paris standards. Naturally it was noisy, narrow, and colorful. It was also unpretentiously very well supplied. I still pay it my respects whenever I am staying in Paris. Its glorious fish and seafood displays—and choice—I still miss a great deal. Finding good seafood or fish in London is an expensive and laborious exercise, reeking of foodie snobbery.

It seems that Paris was always well supplied with fish. When Elizabeth of Austria, the new wife of King Charles IX, first arrived in Paris in 1570, the municipality decided to hold a banquet in her honor. But it was Lent and the Church kept to its rules: No meat was to be allowed. The Queen Mother's fishmongers came to the rescue. No problem. They could guarantee to supply sole, turbot, mullet, trout, carp, pike, lamprey, salmon (fresh and salted), shad, herring, lobsters, crabs, crayfish, mussels, and a thousand frogs. They couldn't quite promise mackerel, sturgeon, porpoise, and tortoise, but they were hopeful . . . Not a bad spread to pick from.

LANGOUSTINES
Dublin Bay Prawns

TRULY A FOOD to feast on. *Langoustines* traditionally feature on the family menu at least once sometime over Christmas and the New Year. Since every other French family tends to do just the same, and prices inevitably rocket a little higher every year, this isn't a particularly bright move in terms of economics. Even apart from Christmas, *langoustines* have always been a family treat. When one member of the family wants to be nice to us all, he or she buys as many crustaceans as the cash flow permits, makes a mayonnaise, and we tuck merrily in—armed with a bottle of Chablis or Alsace Pinot Gris, finger bowls, large napkins, and suitable hardware to extract the last bit of flesh from the claws. Not a pretty sight for outsiders, but plenty of happy memories for the Moines.

There are elaborate ways of cooking *langoustines*, but not in my book. I think they are best either *au naturel* or simply pan-fried. Allow six *langoustines* per person, four at the very least. The heads and shells are worth keeping for making stock. A pinch of saffron is a desirable optional extra.

24 raw, unshelled *langoustines*
1 lemon, cut into wedges, to
   serve

LANGOUSTINES AU NATUREL
⅔ cup (150 ml) dry white wine
sea salt
2 shallots

Serves 4

1 bay leaf
6 tablespoons (90 g) butter, if
   serving hot
⅔ cup (150 ml) mayonnaise
   (see page 13), if serving cold
1 lemon

LANGOUSTINES POÊLÉES
1 tablespoon (15 ml) olive oil
4 tablespoons (60 g) butter
1 shallot
1 clove of garlic
several sprigs of parsley
½ lemon

LANGOUSTINES AU NATUREL

IN A VERY LARGE SAUCEPAN, BRING TO A boil plenty of water, the wine, a generous pinch of salt, the shallots, and the bay leaf. Simmer for a few minutes.

Wash the *langoustines* in cold water. Turn up the heat, bring the liquid back to a fast boil, and add the *langoustines*. Return to a boil and cook for 3 to 5 minutes, depending on size.

Turn off the heat and leave the *langoustines* in the stock for a few minutes; drain, and refresh under cold water. Serve either hot with melted butter, or cold with mayonnaise. Serve with wedges of lemon.

LANGOUSTINES POÊLÉES

COOK THE *LANGOUSTINES* AS BEFORE BUT for 2 minutes only. As soon as they are cool enough to handle, shell them. Start by twisting, or cutting, off the heads. Pull the shell apart, slitting the undersides with scissors if necessary, then holding the tail shell and pulling the meat free. Remove any large dark intestinal threads, rinse, and dry.

Heat the oil and butter in a large sauté pan. Chop the shallot and garlic and soften for a minute. Add the *langoustines* and sauté gently all over 2 to 3 minutes. Snip in the parsley and sprinkle with the juice of ½ lemon. Serve with pan juices and with lemon wedges.

MOULES MARINIÈRE
Mussels in White Wine

A HOMEGROWN COMPROMISE: This version of *moules marinière* includes a little cream, but is not as rich as the roux-and-egg based *moules pulette*.

5 pints or 4 pounds (3 liters or 1.8 kg) mussels in their shells	Serves 4 to 6	7 ounces (200 ml) water sea salt
2 shallots		freshly ground black pepper
1 clove of garlic	a few sprigs of chives	4 tablespoons (60 ml) heavy
4 tablespoons (60 g) butter	a few sprigs of thyme	cream
several sprigs of parsley	1 cup (250 ml) dry white wine	fresh crusty bread, to serve

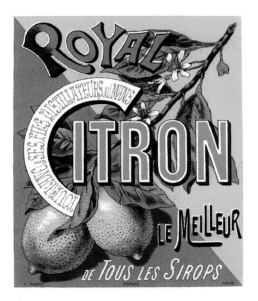

SCRUB THE MUSSELS UNDER COLD RUNNING water and remove the black beards. Discard any mussels that remain open or looked cracked; keep the mussels in plenty of cold water.

Finely chop the shallots and garlic. Melt the butter in a very large saucepan, then add the chopped shallots and garlic, and sweat for a couple of minutes. Snip in the parsley, chives, and thyme, reserving a few sprigs to finish the dish. Pour in the white wine and water and bring to a boil. Reduce the heat and simmer the liquid for a few minutes.

Add the mussels, turn up the heat, and season with very little salt and plenty of black pepper. Cook for 3 to 5 minutes, until the mussels open, shaking the pan occasionally. If any mussels have failed to open, discard them. Remove the mussels with a draining spoon and heap them in a large bowl.

Increase the heat a little, add the cream to the pan, and stir in well. Pour the sauce over the mussels. Snip the rest of the fresh herbs over the mussels and serve at once with plenty of fresh crusty bread.

MOULES FARCIES
Stuffed Mussels

A GLORIOUS DISH. I like my stuffed mussels exceedingly garlicky, but the flavored butter will still be delicious even if you go very easy on the garlic.

Serves 4 to 6

5 pints or 4 pounds (3 liters or 1.8 kg) large, fat mussels in their shells
1 large onion
1 carrot
6½ tablespoons (100 ml) dry white wine
1 bay leaf

a few sprigs each of parsley and thyme
freshly ground black pepper
fresh crusty bread, to serve

FOR THE STUFFING
2 to 4 cloves of garlic
several sprigs of parsley

several sprigs of chives
10 tablespoons (150 g) butter, softened
1 cup (60 g) breadcrumbs made from day-old bread
sea salt
freshly ground black pepper

SCRUB THE MUSSELS WELL WITH A HARD brush under plenty of cold running water and pull off the black beards. Discard any cracked mussels and any that are still open at this stage; keep the mussels in a large bowl of cold water.

Chop the onion and carrot. Pour the wine into a very large saucepan. Add the onion, carrot, bay leaf, parsley, and thyme, then season with a little pepper.

Throw in the mussels and cook over a high heat for a few minutes until the shells open, shaking the pan occasionally. Remove the mussels from the pan with a draining spoon and discard any that are still closed. As soon as they are cool enough to handle,

remove the mussels from their shells. Reserve the mussels and the bottom shells.

Heat the oven to 450°F. Now make the stuffing. Finely chop the garlic and snip the parsley and chives very finely. Using a fork, mash together the soft butter, garlic, parsley, chives, and breadcrumbs. Season with a little salt and plenty of black pepper.

Using a teaspoon or the point of a small knife, put a little flavored butter in each half-shell. Add a mussel, then cover with a good layer of flavored butter. Arrange the mussels in a single layer in a large gratin dish and bake for 6 to 8 minutes, until sizzling brown. Serve the mussels immediately with fresh crusty bread.

SALADE DE MOULES AUX POMMES DE TERRE

Mussels with Potato Salad

A SUBSTANTIAL, BUT happy combination of mussels, potatoes, and mayonnaise.

Serves 6

3 or 4 large waxy potatoes
sea salt
6 tablespoons (90 ml) olive oil
1½ tablespoons (22 ml) white
    or red wine vinegar
2 teaspoons (10 ml) mustard
freshly ground black pepper
5 pints or 4 pounds (3 liters or
    1.8 kg) mussels in their shells

1 large onion
1 carrot
6½ tablespoons (100 ml) dry
    white wine
several sprigs of parsley
a few sprigs of thyme
½ cup (100 ml) mild
    mayonnaise (see page 13)
several sprigs of chives

MAKE THE POTATO SALAD. BRING THE potatoes to a boil in plenty of lightly salted water. Reduce the heat and simmer gently until the potatoes are cooked, but still firm. Drain the potatoes and leave to cool in a colander until you can handle them comfortably. Remove the skins and cut the potatoes into medium-thick slices.

Whisk together the olive oil, vinegar, and mustard. Season liberally with salt and black pepper. Distribute the dressing over the potatoes, and gently turn them over until evenly coated.

Prepare and cook the mussels as described for *moules farcies* (page 63). Lift the mussels out of the cooking liquid with a draining spoon. Stir 1 to 2 tablespoons of the cooking liquid into the mayonnaise, a little at a time. Remove the mussels from their shells and discard the shells; leave to cool. Once the mussels are cold, toss them in the mayonnaise and season with freshly ground black pepper.

Heap the mussels in the center of a round dish. Surround with the potato salad. Chop the parsley and chives and sprinkle over the potato salad. Serve at room temperature.

SOUPE DE MOULES
Mussel Soup

My MOTHER'S RECIPE for mussel soup, full of fragrance. Both mussels and soup can be cooked several hours ahead and assembled at the last minute.

Serves 6

5 pints or 4 pounds (3 liters or 1.8 kg) mussels in their shells
1 large onion
2 carrots
2½ cups (600 ml) dry white wine
1 bay leaf
thyme and parsley, plus extra parsley to finish
freshly ground black pepper
2 leeks

2 shallots
2 tablespoons (30 g) butter
a few saffron strands
3 cups (750 ml) water
1 clove of garlic
6 chunky slices of French bread
olive oil for sprinkling
½ cup (120 ml) light cream
1 extra-large egg yolk
sea salt

Prepare and cook the mussels as described for *moules farcies* (page 63); strain and reserve the cooking liquid. Remove the mussels from their shells as soon as they are cool enough to handle; discard the shells.

Finely chop the leeks and the shallots. Melt the butter in a large saucepan. Add the saffron strands and gently sweat the chopped vegetables without letting them brown. After a few minutes, pour in the remaining 2 cups (500 ml) white wine, the water, and the reserved cooking liquid. Bring to a simmer and cook for a few minutes.

Heat the broiler. In a small bowl, snip the rest of the parsley. Cut the garlic in half and rub the bread with the cut sides of garlic. Sprinkle with olive oil and toast lightly on both sides under the broiler.

Add the mussels to the liquid with half the parsley and return to a simmer. Combine the cream and the egg yolk with 1 tablespoon of the hot liquid. Stir the mixture into the soup. Check the seasoning; this soup needs plenty of freshly ground black pepper. Sprinkle with the remaining parsley and serve at once with the hot garlic toast.

COQUILLES SAINT-JACQUES À LA CRÈME ET AU SAFRAN

Scallops with Saffron Cream

THIS DISH IS more of a main course than the other scallop recipes. Serve with long-grain rice cooked in a light stock.

Serves 4

12 to 16 scallops, off their
   shells
a few sprigs of parsley
2 tablespoons (30 ml) brandy
1 tablespoon (15 ml) olive oil
2 tablespoons (30 g) butter

a pinch of powdered saffron
7 ounces (200 ml) sour cream
1 egg yolk
sea salt
cayenne pepper

RINSE THE SCALLOPS UNDER COLD running water, and remove any gristle and black threads. Separate the orange coral from the white flesh, and cut the flesh into 2 or 3 disks, depending on the size of the scallops. Snip the parsley into a small bowl. Put the prepared scallops and corals in a soup plate, sprinkle with brandy, cover, and marinate for at least 30 minutes, turning the scallops over once or twice.

Heat the oil and butter in a sauté pan. Drain the scallops and collect the brandy juices; reserve the corals. Gently cook the slices of scallop flesh with three-quarters of the parsley in the hot oil and butter for 2 minutes, just long enough for the scallops to change color and become firmer. Turn the

scallops over once or twice during cooking. Remove them from the pan with a pancake turner; set aside.

Now mash half the corals in a small bowl. Stir the saffron into the hot fat, then add the mashed corals, the cream, and the brandy. Bring to a boil and simmer for a couple of minutes, stirring frequently, then add the rest of the corals and cook for another minute.

Beat the egg yolk with 2 tablespoons of the hot saffron cream. Stir into the pan and reduce the heat–the mixture should no longer be allowed to boil. Continue stirring for a minute or so, then add the reserved scallop slices. Heat through, and season lightly with salt and cayenne. Sprinkle with the rest of the parsley and serve.

COQUILLES SAINT-JACQUES AU BEURRE BLANC

Scallops with Shallot Butter

A CLASSIC WAY of preparing scallops, and one of my favorites. The only problem is that this recipe does require constant attention. You can make the *court bouillon* and reduce the shallots well in advance, but after that, allow a totally uninterrupted quarter of an hour at the stove. The sauce will keep warm for a few minutes over hot water, but the scallops will cool quickly.

Serves 4

8 to 12 scallops, off their shells
1 onion
4 shallots
1 cup (250 ml) dry white wine
1¼ cups (300 ml) water
1 bouquet garni
sea salt
freshly ground black pepper
4 tablespoons (60 ml) white
   wine vinegar
14 tablespoons (210 g) butter
a few sprigs of parsley and
   chives (optional)

MAKE A LIGHT *COURT BOUILLON*. CHOP THE onion and one of the shallots, and bring to a boil in a sauté pan with the white wine, water, and bouquet garni. Season and simmer for 10 minutes. Strain the liquid into a bowl; discard the onion, shallot, and bouquet garni. Return the liquid to the pan.

Start preparing the shallot butter sauce. Very finely chop the rest of the shallots. Cook, with the vinegar, in a small saucepan on a moderate heat until soft and syrupy—this will take a good 15 minutes. Cut the butter into small pieces.

Rinse the scallops under cold running water, remove any gristle and black threads. Separate the orange coral from the white flesh and cut the flesh into 2 or 3 disks, depending on the size of the scallops. Add the scallops, the white flesh first, the corals after 1 minute, to the simmering liquid and

cook very gently for a few minutes—again this will depend on size, but usually 2 to 3 minutes. If the scallops aren't entirely covered by the liquid, add extra water, very hot but not boiling; do not let boil and be careful not to overcook the scallops, since this will toughen the flesh and damage the corals. Reserve 3 tablespoons of the cooking liquid. Drain the scallops and keep warm.

Meanwhile, continue cooking the sauce. Whisk the butter into the shallot purée, a few pieces at a time, without ever letting the mixture come to a boil. Whisk briskly and continuously, occasionally taking the pan off the heat. Trickle the reserved cooking liquid, a little at a time, into the finished sauce, whisking well. Check the seasoning. Snip some parsley and chives into the sauce, if you like. Spoon the sauce over the scallops just before serving.

Coquilles Saint-Jacques Surprise
Scallops with a Puff Pastry Lid

I CANNOT REMEMBER exactly where I first ate this dish. All I remember is that it was a long time ago, in someone's house, and with my parents . . . I like serving seafood first courses in scallop shells and the puff pastry lids are fun to break into.
The method also works well with folded fillets of sole or turbot, perhaps with the addition of a small pinch of saffron.

8 to 12 scallops, and 4 large, undamaged, saucer-shaped scallop shells	Serves 4	2 tablespoons (30 g) butter sea salt
1 shallot		cayenne pepper
7 ounces (200 g) button mushrooms	4 tablespoons (60 ml) dry white wine	a little flour 10 ounces (300 g) store-bought puff pastry dough
1 tablespoon (15 ml) olive oil	several sprigs of chives	1 egg yolk

RINSE THE SCALLOPS WELL UNDER COLD running water. Remove the grayish gristle around the cushion and the black threads, then separate the coral from the white flesh and cut the flesh into 2 or 3 disks, depending on the size of the scallops. Wash the scallop shells, scrubbing them if necessary; dry well.

Steam the prepared scallops for 2 to 3 minutes over boiling water. Meanwhile, finely chop the shallot. Wipe the mushrooms and slice very thinly. Heat the oil and soften the shallot and mushrooms for a couple of minutes over a low heat. Put a baking sheet in the oven and heat to 425°F.

Divide the shallot and mushroom mixture among the prepared shells. Cover with slices of scallop and coral. Moisten with the white wine and snip in some chives. Add a small knob of butter and season lightly with salt and cayenne.

On a lightly floured board, roll out the dough very thinly. Cut into 4 circles, slightly larger than the scallop shells. Place a dough "lid" over each filled scallop shell. Score the dough attractively with a sharp knife, and make a hole in the center to let the steam escape. Now seal the dough: Press the edges down all the way around with moistened fingers, to seal, and then brush the edges with a little egg yolk.

Bake for 1 minute, then remove from the oven and brush all over the pastry lids lightly with egg yolk to glaze. Bake for 7 to 8 minutes more. Serve immediately.

SAUMON CUIT AU FOUR AVEC UNE PETITE SAUCE SAFRANÉE

Roast Salmon with Saffron Sauce

ALL IT TAKES FOR A NEW DISH to become part of the family repertoire is one happy feast, with empty platters and plates scraped clean at the end of it. A few summers ago we celebrated July 14th and France's soccer World Cup success with a huge oven-roasted flounder served with saffrony juices. It had a price tag to match its size. Our favorite fishmonger in the local market (the one whose stall attracts the longest line) still grins at us fondly every time he sees us approach. *Un beau fletan?* What about a nice flounder, he asks invitingly . . . More often than not we leave with somewhat humbler fry in the still handsome shape of a salmon or sea trout, both particularly good cooked this way.

If you do succumb to a flounder, roast it dark skin up for 20 to 30 minutes, until barely flaky, checking after 20 minutes lest you overcook this precious beauty.

Serves 6

1 salmon, about 3 pounds (1.4 kg), head removed, drawn, boned, and halved lengthwise	leaves from several sprigs of rosemary and parsley, snipped	2 tablespoons (60 g) butter, diced
3 tablespoons (45 ml) olive oil	white parts of 3 large scallions, thinly sliced	a pinch of saffron strands
	1 unwaxed lemon, half juiced, half thinly sliced	sea salt
		freshly ground black pepper

HEAT THE OVEN TO 400°F. RUB THE SKIN of the salmon with salt and pepper, then brush with a little olive oil. Brush the roasting pan with olive oil, then scatter some of the herbs and half of the lemon slices in the center of the pan. Distribute the scallion evenly over the top. Then put the salmon on top of the scallion, flesh sides up.

Paint the flesh side of the fish with olive oil. Scatter over a few more herbs, then season with salt and pepper. Dot a quarter of the butter over the salmon, sprinkle with half the lemon juice, and season again.

Roast for about 20 minutes, until the salmon is opaque and cooked through to your liking.

Meanwhile, bring about 7 ounces (200 ml) water to a boil. Leave the fish to settle for 5 minutes, then, using a pancake turner, transfer the salmon to a warm serving dish, skin side down. Put the roasting pan over a moderate heat (or pour the cooking juices into a small saucepan if your pan is not flameproof). Add the lemon juice and saffron strands, and stir for a minute. Stir in the boiling water and continue stirring for a few seconds. Add the rest of the butter, and whisk in. Season the sauce and strain into a warmed sauceboat. Spoon a couple of tablespoons of sauce over the salmon. Decorate with the rest of the herbs and lemon slices, and serve as soon as possible.

Soupe de Poissons Madame Bastier
A Provençal Fish Soup

Cherchez le poisson—it's not easy to get *rascasse, girelles,* and *sarans* away from the Mediterranean shores. I use a mixture of red mullet, brill, smoked cod (for its strong flavor), large shrimp, monkfish, and crab flesh. An extra pinch of saffron will help if you feel your ingredients are too bland.

about 3 pounds (1.5 kg) fish, cleaned, drawn, and chopped, and shellfish (see above)	Serves 4	sea salt freshly ground black pepper
2 large white onions	2 to 3 tablespoons (30 to 45 ml) olive oil	To serve
3 cloves of garlic	½ teaspoon (3 g) ground saffron	pieces of toast rubbed with garlic (see recipe for *soupe de moules* page 65)
1 bulb of fennel	a bunch of thyme	*rouille* (page 29)
1 or 2 potatoes	2 sprigs of rosemary	
2 large ripe tomatoes		

Prepare the vegetables. Chop the onions, garlic, and fennel. Peel and slice the potatoes. Blanch, peel, seed, and chop the tomatoes.

In a heavy-bottomed Dutch oven or large saucepan, heat the oil and gently sauté the onions, garlic, and fennel until very lightly browned. Stir in the fish and cook for a few minutes, then add about 1¼ quarts (1.2 liters) water, the potatoes, saffron, thyme, rosemary, and tomatoes. Bring to a boil, then reduce the heat and simmer for 20 to 25 minutes, until the potatoes are cooked.

Now comes the slightly messy bit of the recipe. Remove the fish and vegetable pieces from the pan with a draining spoon; pick out and discard as much skin, bones, and sprigs of herbs as you can and pass the rest through a *mouli*—or whizz in a food processor. Return to the heat and finish cooking for 5 to 10 minutes. Season and serve with toast rubbed with garlic and *rouille*.

COLIN POÊLÉ SAUCE MOUTARDE
Pan-Fried Cod with Mustard Sauce

FRIDAY WAS, AND STILL is, Fish Day in France. As goodish Catholics we religiously ate fish, but my Protestant cousins on my father's side had fish too, and so did all my school friends. Perhaps it was because the fishmongers' displays were always at their shimmery best on Fridays . . .

I used to beg for sole and *langoustines*. Too expensive, said my mother. Cod was much better value and it duly appeared on the table practically every Friday lunchtime. It was pan-fried, but, alas, not accompanied by mustard sauce. I only liked the "burned bits" and considered the dish to be the height of boring family food. It took me years, and a nice down-to-earth fishmonger's in London's Brewer Street, to enjoy cod. Pity this reliable fish had by then become so expensive. The mustard sauce is a personal favorite, evolved from a recipe my mother was very fond of. I use it with all kinds of fish, poached, broiled, or pan-fried, and it is pretty good with white meat, too.

4 cod steaks	**Serves 4**	1 cup (250 ml) heavy cream
1 tablespoon (15 g) flour	FOR THE MUSTARD SAUCE	1 to 1½ tablespoons (15 to
sea salt	2 shallots	22 ml) Dijon mustard
cayenne pepper	1 small bunch of flat-leaf	sea salt
dried thyme	parsley	freshly ground black pepper
1 tablespoon (15 ml) olive oil	4 tablespoons (60 g) butter	1 egg yolk
2 tablespoons (30 g) butter	1 tablespoon (15 g) flour	½ lemon

DRY THE COD WITH PAPER TOWELS. Season the flour with a little salt, cayenne pepper, and a pinch of dried thyme.

Prepare the mustard sauce. Finely chop the shallots and snip the parsley. Melt half the butter in a small, heavy-bottomed saucepan. Sweat the shallots and parsley in the melted butter over a low heat, making sure neither butter nor shallots change color. Stir in the rest of the butter, then sprinkle in the flour as soon as it has melted. Cook for a couple of minutes, stirring briskly, then add the cream. Continue to cook until thick and smooth, then stir in the mustard. Taste and season well with salt and freshly ground black pepper.

Meanwhile, cook the fish. Heat the oil in a skillet large enough to take the cod steaks comfortably. Add the butter and once it has melted, add the fish. Pan-fry the cod for about 4 minutes on each side, depending on thickness, keeping the heat moderate: The fish tends to disintegrate if you cook it too fast or too long. Turn it over carefully halfway through with a pancake turner.

Just before you are ready to serve, beat the egg yolk with the juice of the ½ lemon in a small bowl. Add 2 tablespoons of the sauce, beat until combined, then stir the mixture into the saucepan. If the sauce seems too thick at this stage, thin it down with a few teaspoons of boiling water, stirred in 1 teaspoon at a time. Arrange the cod steaks on a serving dish. Spoon some of the sauce over them and sprinkle with snipped parsley. Serve the rest of the sauce separately.

COLIN POÊLÉ PETITE SAUCE MOUTARDE
Cod Steaks with Quick-Mustard Sauce

A QUICKIE VERSION of the previous recipe. More basic, certainly, but lighter and a good simple dish.

4 cod steaks
1 tablespoon (15 g) flour
sea salt
cayenne pepper
dried thyme
1 tablespoon (15 ml) olive oil
2 tablespoons (30 g) butter

Serves 4

FOR THE QUICK-MUSTARD SAUCE
6 tablespoons (90 ml) dry white
wine
6 tablespoons (90 ml) heavy
cream

2 tablespoons (30 g) butter
2 to 3 teaspoons (10 to 15 ml)
Dijon mustard
sea salt
freshly ground black pepper
a few sprigs of flat-leaf
parsley

COOK THE FISH AS IN THE PREVIOUS recipe. Remove from the skillet with a pancake turner and keep warm in the serving dish. Turn up the heat a little. Swirl the wine into the pan, then whisk in the cream and stir as the liquid reduces a little.

Cut the butter into small pieces. Stir the mustard into the sauce. Dot the butter pieces around the pan and stir until melted. Season with salt and freshly ground black pepper. Pour or spoon the sauce over the fish and snip the parsley over it. Serve immediately.

RAIE AU BEURRE NOIR
Skate in Black Butter

As I AM ONLY TOO AWARE, there is one slight problem with this justly famous dish: Only a few seconds separate *beurre noir*, which is a tempting hazelnut color, from acrid *beurre brûlé*. The only thing you can do is tip the evil stuff out, pat the pan clean with a wad of paper towels, and start again.

2¼ pounds (1 kg) skate wings
6 tablespoons (90 ml) red wine
vinegar
a few sprigs of thyme
1 bay leaf

Serves 4

1 small onion, quartered
1 small carrot, quartered
sea salt

freshly ground black pepper
several sprigs of parsley
8 tablespoons (120 g) butter
3 tablespoons (45 g) capers

POACH THE FISH. PLACE THE SKATE WINGS in a sauté pan large enough to take the wings comfortably. Cover with cold water, then add 2 tablespoons of vinegar, the thyme, bay leaf, onion, and carrot. Season lightly with salt and freshly ground black pepper, and bring to a boil over a low heat, then simmer gently for 10 to 12 minutes, until the flesh is just tender enough to flake with a fork.

Snip the parsley into a bowl and melt the butter over a very low heat. Remove the skate from the pan with a pancake turner, drain, and

remove the skin if necessary. Pat the flesh dry with paper towels. Put the fish on a serving dish and sprinkle with the parsley; reserve a little poaching liquid.

Turn up the heat under the butter just a little and swirl the butter until it turns golden brown. Trickle half of it over the skate and parsley. Return the pan to the heat, swirl in the rest of the vinegar, the capers, and a couple of tablespoons of poaching liquid. Stir until heated through, pour over the fish, and serve.

LOTTE À LA PROVENÇALE
Monkfish with Tomato and Herbs

THIS UNPRETENTIOUS DISH was definitely inspired by Provence, but I cannot guarantee that it is one hundred percent authentic . . . Use plenty of fresh herbs and very ripe tomatoes.

1¾ pounds (800 g) monkfish, without skin and bones	Serves 4	a few sprigs of rosemary sea salt
1 large white Spanish onion	2 cloves of garlic	freshly ground black pepper
6 tablespoons (90 ml) olive oil	a small bunch of parsley	⅔ cup (150 ml) dry white wine
4 ripe tomatoes	a few sprigs of fresh thyme	2 ounces (60 g) Gruyère cheese

CUT THE FISH INTO 8 TO 10 EVEN-SIZE pieces; pat dry with paper towels. Finely chop the onion. Heat the oven to 350°F.

Heat half the oil in a large skillet. Briskly sauté the fish with half the chopped onion over a moderately high heat, turning the pieces over carefully; the monkfish will soon become firmer and golden white.

Coat a large baking dish with the remaining oil. Remove the monkfish· and onion from the pan with a pancake turner and put them in the dish. Blanch the tomatoes, then peel and slice them thinly; discard the seeds. Arrange the tomato slices over the fish.

Finely chop the garlic. In a small bowl, snip the fresh herbs, reserving a few sprigs of parsley to finish off the dish. Add the rest of the onion and the garlic to the fresh herbs and stir well. Scatter the mixture over the fish and tomatoes. Season with salt and black pepper and pour in the wine. Grate the cheese over the dish.

Bake for 15 to 20 minutes until sizzling and golden brown. Snip the rest of the parsley over the dish and serve hot.

GRATIN DE HADDOCK AU RIZ
Gratin of Smoked Haddock

I STILL HAVE my mother's index card with her blueprint of this recipe, in her precise and elegant handwriting. She wasn't at all convinced when I told her I thought *gratin de haddock au riz* was rather like an Anglo-Indian classic called kedgeree . . . The basic ingredients may be similar, but the cheesy *gratin* method and the end result are definitely very French.

Serves 4

1¾ pounds (800 g) skinned
    smoked haddock fillets
5 cups (1.2 liters) milk
4 tablespoons (60 g) butter
grated nutmeg
1 egg
generous 1 cup (225 g) long-
    grain rice
sea salt
3 ounces (90 g) Gruyère or
    sharp cheddar
3 tablespoons (45 g)
    breadcrumbs made from
    day-old bread
a small bunch of parsley
freshly ground black pepper

RINSE THE HADDOCK. IN A SAUCEPAN wide enough to take the haddock fillets side by side, bring the milk to a simmer with a knob of butter and a good pinch of nutmeg. Hard-boil, and then shell the egg. Meanwhile, add the haddock to the milk and poach for 5 to 8 minutes, until firm and just cooked. Lift out of the pan with a draining spoon and drain; set aside on paper towels. Reserve the milk in the pan.

Cook the rice in another saucepan for 3 minutes in lightly salted boiling water. Bring the milk back to a boil. Drain the rice and pour it into the boiling milk. Reduce the heat a little and simmer for 15 minutes, or until the rice is tender.

Heat the oven to 400°F. Butter a baking dish. Drain, refresh, and again drain the rice, then spread it over the dish bottom; pat dry with a paper towel. Grate half the cheese over the rice. Shred the haddock, removing all the bones you can spot, and spread the flakes over the rice and grated cheese.

Grate the rest of the cheese over the haddock. Sprinkle with the breadcrumbs, then snip the parsley and scatter most of it over the dish, reserving a little. Dot with small pieces of butter. Season with black pepper and bake for 5 to 10 minutes, until crisp and golden. Grate the hard-boiled egg into the bowl with the reserved parsley. Mix and sprinkle over the dish before serving.

Brandade de Morue
Salt Cod Purée

Perhaps it was because the village church wasn't heated, but, as a child, I always found Good Friday a shivery experience. The happiness of Easter Sunday seemed an intolerably long way away. The warmest thing about Good Friday was *brandade de morue*, smooth, creamy, pleasingly fishy, and very comforting. The recipe below is the one I prefer. When I cooked *brandade* for my father, who had a marked fondness for *crème fraîche*, I used double the amount of cream to avoid complaints—and the irritating sight of a large undistinguished tub being ostentatiously passed around the table.

1 pound (450 g) salt cod	Serves 4 to 6	freshly ground black pepper
1 bouquet garni		garlic croutons, to serve, if
3 cloves of garlic		liked
7 ounces (200 ml) olive oil	3 tablespoons (45 ml) heavy	butter to reheat, if wished
6½ tablespoons (100 ml) milk	cream	

Soak the salt cod for at least 18 hours in plenty of cold water, changing the water several times.

Break the fish into several chunks. Place in a sauté pan with the bouquet garni, cover with cold water, bring to a boil, and simmer for 10 minutes; remove from the pan and drain well. Discard the skin and as many bones as possible, and shred the salt cod very finely into a large bowl. Finely chop the garlic and gently heat the olive oil and milk in separate pans.

Put the bowl of shredded salt cod over a pan of simmering water. Gradually pour in half the warm olive oil, pounding the mixture well with a large pestle or wooden spoon. Work in the garlic, then the rest of the oil and the warm milk, a little at a time—this will take about 10 minutes and you should end up with a thick, slightly sticky, white purée.

Stir in the cream and season generously with freshly ground black pepper. Serve at once, if you like with garlic croutons. Alternatively, leave to cool completely.

To reheat, generously butter a gratin dish and spoon the *brandade* into the dish. Smooth the top, and dot with butter. Reheat in the oven at 375°F for 15 minutes or so before serving the dish.

Morue Parmentier
Salt Cod with Potatoes

This dish requires less elbow grease than *brandade de morue*. Make sure you poach the cod very gently since it tends to toughen when boiled too fast or for too long.

Serves 4 to 6

1 pound (450 g) salt cod
1 pound (450 g) waxy potatoes
sea salt
1 bouquet garni
1 large white onion
1 tablespoon (15 ml) olive oil
7 ounces (200 ml) béchamel
  (see page 13)
butter for greasing and to finish
cayenne pepper
⅓ cup (45 g) grated Gruyère or
  sharp cheddar cheese
several sprigs of parsley,
  chopped
freshly ground black pepper

Soak the salt cod in plenty of cold water for at least 18 hours, changing the water several times. Cook the potatoes in barely boiling, lightly salted water until just tender. Drain, refresh, and peel the potatoes as soon as they are cool enough to handle; cut them into thick slices.

While the potatoes are boiling, poach the salt cod. Break it into chunks, place in a sauté pan with the bouquet garni, cover with cold water, and bring to a boil, then simmer gently for 10 minutes; drain well. Discard as much skin and bones as possible, then shred the cod.

Heat the oven to 400°F. Finely chop the onion. Heat the oil in a small skillet and sweat the onion over a low heat for a few minutes, stirring frequently. Remove from the pan with a draining spoon, drain on paper towels, then stir the onion into the béchamel.

Butter a gratin dish. Spread the slices of potato over the dish. Cover with the shredded salt cod and season with a little cayenne pepper. Cover with the onion-flavored béchamel. Scatter the cheese and parsley over the béchamel. Season with freshly ground black pepper, and dot with butter. Bake until golden brown. Serve hot.

MORUE EN AÏOLI
Salt Cod with Garlic Mayonnaise

VARY THE VEGETABLES according to what is in season. Cooked beets are a popular accompaniment.

2¼ pounds (1 kg) salt cod	Serves 6	several sprigs of thyme
4 eggs		2 bay leaves
8 small potatoes		1 onion
sea salt		⅔ cup (150 ml) dry white wine
4 carrots		1½ cups (350 ml) garlic
3 bulbs of fennel		mayonnaise (see page 13)
1 small cauliflower		2 tomatoes
14 ounces (400 g) green beans		freshly ground black pepper

SOAK THE SALT COD IN PLENTY OF COLD water for at least 18 hours, changing the water several times.

Once the fish is de-salted, hard-boil the eggs and start preparing the vegetables. Scrub the potatoes, then cook them in lightly salted water. Peel the carrots, cut them into chunks, and cook in lightly salted boiling water. Trim and halve the fennel bulbs and cook with the carrots. Cut the cauliflower into florets and cook in lightly salted water. Top and tail the beans and cook with the cauliflower florets. The vegetables should all be cooked through but not soft. Refresh them quickly under cold running water and drain well.

Now poach the fish. Break the cod into chunks. Place in a large sauté pan with the thyme, bay leaves, onion, and wine. Cover with cold water, bring to a boil, turn the heat down, and simmer very gently for 12 to 15 minutes, until the fish is just tender. Remove the fish from the pan, drain well, refresh, and drain again; discard the skin and bones and coarsely shred the fish. Beat 1 to 2 tablespoons of the poaching liquid into the garlic mayonnaise.

Arrange the shredded salt cold in the center of a large serving dish. Shell the hard-boiled eggs and cut them in half lengthwise. Quarter and seed the tomatoes. Arrange the tomatoes and eggs around the salt cod. Surround with the cooked vegetables.

To finish, season the dish with a little freshly ground black pepper and serve with a bowl of garlic mayonnaise.

FILETS DE MERLAN AUX PETITS LÉGUMES

Baked Whiting Fillets with Vegetables

WHITING MAY NOT be many people's favorite fish, but it responds very well to the treatment below. This is a good method for cooking all the humbler varieties of whitefish. You will also find whiting labeled as silver hake.

Serves 4

7 ounces (200 g) carrots
4 ounces (120 g) celery
7 ounces (200 g) cremini
   (brown cap) mushrooms
2 shallots
3 tablespoons (45 g) butter
sea salt
freshly ground black pepper
5 ounces (150 ml) light cream
6 whiting fillets, skinned
½ cup (120 ml) dry white wine
a few sprigs of chervil
a few sprigs of chives

PREPARE THE VEGETABLES. PEEL THE carrots, and slice into small matchsticks. Trim the celery and cut into narrow slices. Halve and finely slice the mushrooms. Finely chop the shallots.

In a sauté pan, melt half the butter and gently cook the carrots, celery, and mushrooms over a low heat for about 10 minutes, stirring occasionally. Season with salt and black pepper and stir in half the cream. Cook, partly covered, for 5 minutes more, still over a low heat; do not let boil.

Heat the oven to 350°F. Spread the vegetables out in a baking dish large enough to hold the whiting in a single layer; put the fillets on top of the vegetables. Sprinkle with the chopped shallots and trickle the white wine and the rest of the cream over the fish. Season lightly with salt and more generously with black pepper. Dot with the remaining butter and bake for 15 to 20 minutes, or until just cooked.

Snip the fresh herbs over the fish and serve hot.

TRUITE AUX PIGNONS
Trout with Pine Nuts

AN EASY VARIATION, which I particularly like, on the well-known theme of trout with almonds.

	Serves 4	
1 lemon		freshly ground black pepper
4 trout, cleaned and drawn		½ cup (60 g) pine nuts
a few sprigs of thyme	2 tablespoons (30 ml) olive oil	3 tablespoons (45 g) butter
a few sprigs of marjoram	sea salt	3 tablespoons (45 ml) dry white wine

HEAT THE OVEN TO 375°F. CUT THE lemon in half, then cut one half into 4 slices and squeeze the other half. Cut 4 pieces of foil large enough to envelop the trout.

Place a trout in the center of each piece of foil. Put a little thyme and marjoram inside each trout, then sprinkle the cavity with a few drops of olive oil and season with salt and freshly ground black pepper. Place a slice of lemon on each trout, sprinkle with a few pine nuts and a little olive oil and lemon juice. Season lightly.

Wrap the foil around the fish, and seal well. Bake for 15 to 20 minutes, until the flesh is just tender enough to flake.

Meanwhile, melt a knob of butter in a small skillet and sauté the rest of the pine nuts until golden. Remove from the pan with a draining spoon and drain on paper towels. Swirl the white wine into the pan, add the rest of the butter and stir until melted. Open the foil packages a little, sprinkle in the fried pine nuts, and trickle in a little wine and butter sauce. Serve immediately.

TRUITE AUX CHAMPIGNONS
Trout with Mushrooms

A RECIPE BORROWED from another happy French exile in London, Marie-France Sandon. I have often prepared trout in this pleasingly different way since first tasting it at Marie-France's.

	Serves 4	
4 ounces (120 g) button mushrooms		sea salt
4 shallots	2 bay leaves	freshly ground black pepper
several sprigs of fresh thyme	7 ounces (200 ml) beer or	4 trout, cleaned and drawn
several sprigs of parsley	light ale	⅔ cup (150 ml) light cream

WIPE AND THINLY SLICE THE MUSHROOMS, then chop the shallots very finely. In a sauté pan large enough to take the trout in a single layer, spread out the mushrooms and shallots. Add the thyme, parsley, and bay leaves, reserving some parsley. Moisten with the beer and season with salt and freshly ground black pepper. Bring to a boil, lower the heat and simmer for about 10 minutes.

Add the fish to the pan, with just enough water to cover. Return to a simmer and poach for 10 minutes over a gentle heat, until the fish is tender enough to flake with a fork. Remove from the pan with a pancake turner; drain and put on a serving dish.

Turn up the heat and boil the poaching liquid until it is reduced to about half the original quantity; discard the sprigs of herbs and the bay leaves. Stir in the cream until heated through. Pour the sauce over the fish. Snip the rest of the parsley over the dish, season again, and serve immediately.

DAURADE FARCIE AUX AMANDES
Sea Bream with Almond Stuffing

WHAT A CONSUMER-FRIENDLY fish the sea bream is, with its firm flesh and untreacherous bones. This is a fun dish to make. The stuffing can be prepared ahead and chilled, leaving only the little surgical job and the finishing touches to do before baking. The cooked fish will stay hot enough for a good 20 minutes in the oven if need be, but cut back on the cooking time a little.

2 eggs
4 tablespoons (60 ml) milk
1 thick slice of bread without
   the crust
1 large white Spanish onion
1 shallot
1 clove of garlic
3 tablespoons (45 ml) olive oil,
   plus extra if necessary

Serves 4 to 6

about 24 fresh shelled almonds
several sprigs of parsley
a few sprigs of thyme
a sprig of rosemary
1 bay leaf

sea salt
freshly ground black pepper
¾ cup (45 g) breadcrumbs
   made from day-old bread
1 sea bream weighing about
   1¾ pounds (800 g)
3 tablespoons (45 g) butter
⅔ cup (150 ml) dry white wine,
   plus extra if necessary

PREPARE THE STUFFING. HARD-BOIL AND shell 1 egg. Heat the milk to boiling point in a small saucepan and soak the bread until cool enough to handle. Drain and squeeze with your hands to get rid of the excess moisture. Combine the onion with the shallot and garlic in a food processor. Heat 1 tablespoon of olive oil and sauté the mixture for a few minutes over a low heat, stirring frequently.

Without rinsing the bowl of the food processor, whizz half the almonds until finely ground. Add the parsley, thyme, rosemary, bay leaf, hard-boiled egg, and bread and whizz, then moisten with the remaining egg. Add the sautéed onion, season lightly with salt and black pepper, and whizz again.

Heat the oven to 375°F. Slit the belly of the fish open with a sharp knife. Wipe the cavity with paper towels, then spoon in the stuffing: The stuffing will expand during cooking, so don't pack the cavity too tightly. Sew up the slit to secure the stuffing. Coat a large baking dish with 1 tablespoon of olive oil. Put the fish in the dish and spoon any remaining stuffing around it. Brush the fish with the rest of the oil and sprinkle with the breadcrumbs. Cut the rest of the almonds into slivers and scatter them over the fish. Cut the butter into small pieces and dot all over. Moisten with the white wine.

Cover the dish with foil and bake for 40 to 50 minutes, basting a few times with the cooking juices: If the dish looks too dry, add extra wine and a little more olive oil. After about 30 minutes, remove the foil to let the topping turn golden brown. Remove the thread that held the stuffing in place and serve piping hot.

TERRINE DE POISSONS ANNE-SOPHIE
Sole and Salmon Terrine

COLD FISH TERRINES make good first courses for large family reunions, when you want to serve something reasonably impressive but have precious little time at the last minute. My sister's handsome dish is a reliable favorite. You can process the herbs for the sauce a little ahead, but don't whisk up the sauce until you are nearly ready to sit people down at the table.

Serves 8 to 10

3 tablespoons (45 g) butter
3 small sole, skinned and filleted
1½ pounds (750 g) salmon steaks, skinned and boned
oil for greasing
12 large shrimp in their shells, to finish the dish
a few sprigs of parsley or watercress, to finish the dish

FOR THE STUFFING
1 cup (250 ml) milk
½ cup (30 g) fresh white breadcrumbs
1 pound (450 g) whiting or cod, skinned and boned
10 tablespoons (150 g) butter
2 eggs
12 egg yolks
2¼ cups (550 ml) heavy cream or *crème fraîche*
2 tablespoons (30 ml) brandy
sea salt

freshly ground black pepper
grated nutmeg
ground cayenne pepper

FOR THE SAUCE
a large bunch of watercress
several sprigs each of parsley, chives, and chervil
1¼ cups (300 ml) *crème fraîche*
½ lemon
freshly ground black pepper

MELT THE BUTTER IN A LARGE SKILLET and gently sauté the sole fillets and salmon steaks, a few at a time, over a low heat; leave to cool completely. Meanwhile, prepare the stuffing. Bring the milk to a boil in a small saucepan, then stir in the breadcrumbs. Reduce the heat and let the mixture thicken a little, stirring it occasionally.

Chop the whiting finely in a food processor, then add the butter, eggs and egg yolks, and the milk mixture, and process until smooth. Tip or spoon the mixture into a large bowl, and whisk in the cream, a little at a time. Trickle in the brandy, still stirring. Season lightly with salt and more generously with freshly ground black pepper. Stir in a good pinch of nutmeg and a small pinch of cayenne pepper

Heat the oven to 400°F. Grease a 2-quart (2.5-liter) bread pan. Line the bottom with sole fillets, spread in a layer of stuffing, then a layer of salmon. Continue alternating layers, ending with a layer of stuffing. Knock

the pan a couple of times on the counter to ensure it is well packed.

Line a large roasting pan with a folded newspaper. Put the bread pan in the center of the roasting pan. Pour in the boiling water until it comes halfway up the sides of the bread pan and cook the terrine in this *bain-marie* for approximately 1 hour, until the top of the terrine feels firm. Leave the terrine to get cool, then cover and weigh it down. Refrigerate for at least 3 hours, or up to 48 hours if you wish.

Prepare the sauce. Wash and trim the watercress and herbs; drain well and process quickly. Just before serving, whisk the *crème fraîche* in a bowl, then gradually stir in the herb mixture, whisking it well in. Squeeze in the lemon juice. Season the sauce with little black pepper and spoon it into a sauceboat. Now unmold the terrine into the center of a large serving dish. Surround with the shrimp and sprigs of parsley or watercress. Serve with the sauce.

PAINS DE POISSON
Fish Loaves

In President de Gaulle's brave new France circa 1960, modern women like my mother, ex-career girls now full-time wives and mothers, were busy swopping colorful recipes that were at the time a little daring—in their relaxed use of canned food, spices, and foreign, exotic ingredients. *Plats uniques* became the "in thing" for dinner parties, with *paella* playing a starring role.

The following fish loaves are typical of the period. There was a sharp difference between family food—thrifty, filling but experimental—and dishes for entertaining—elaborately garnished and evidently more expensive. The basic fish loaf recipe was purely for family use. Note that it lists ketchup among its ingredients, the first recorded use of the stuff in my homegrown cards. Fish loaf and assorted jokes about yet another biblical miracle on the shores of the Loire became a family institution.

The second recipe was *pour les invités*—for guests. I still prefer it to the basic dish, but, then, wouldn't I just?

PAIN DE POISSON DE TOUS LES JOURS
Family Fish Loaf

Serves 6

1 pound (450 g) whitefish,
  skinned and boned
1 bay leaf
1 bouquet garni
sea salt
freshly ground black pepper
2 ounces (60 g) tomato paste
  (purée)
2 tablespoons (30 ml) tomato
  ketchup
5 eggs
paprika
cayenne pepper
oil for greasing
4 tablespoons (60 g) butter

Put the fish with the bay leaf and bouquet garni in a sauté pan. Cover with cold water, season with salt and freshly ground black pepper, and bring to a boil, then simmer until the flesh is tender enough to flake easily. Drain well, remove any bones, and put through a *mouli* or food processor. Stir in the tomato paste and ketchup.

Beat the eggs as for an omelet. Stir them into the fish mixture until well blended. Season with a good pinch of paprika and cayenne.

Heat the oven to 350°F. Grease a large bread pan, about 3 quarts (2.5 liters). Pour the mixture into the pan. Line a large roasting pan with a folded newspaper. Put the bread pan in the center of the roasting pan. Pour boiling water to come halfway up the sides of the bread pan and cook the fish loaf in this *bain-marie* for 40 minutes, or until firm.

Unmold the fish loaf onto a dish. Melt the butter in a small saucepan and pour over the fish loaf just before serving. Delicious with *anchoïade* (see page 35).

Pain de Poisson pour Invités
Posh Fish Loaf

2 large white Spanish onions
3 tablespoons (45 ml) olive oil,
    plus extra for greasing
2¼ pounds (1 kg) tomatoes
1 clove of garlic
several sprigs of thyme,
    marjoram, and parsley
dried oregano
4 pounds (1.8 kg) cod or hake,
    skinned and boned

Serves 8

3 thin slices of cooked ham
1⅓ cups (200 g) green olives,
    pitted
5 or 6 eggs

sea salt
freshly ground black pepper
paprika
cayenne pepper
2 red bell peppers

To serve
8 tablespoons (120 g) butter
½ lemon or 1½ cups (350 ml)
    hollandaise (see page 12)

Prepare a tomato sauce. Chop the onions. Heat 1 tablespoon olive oil in a skillet and sauté the onions over a low heat, stirring frequently. Blanch, skin, halve, and seed the tomatoes, then chop roughly with the garlic and add to the onions. Add the herbs and cook gently for 20 to 30 minutes. Remove the sprigs of herbs from the pan, then process the sauce in a food processor or put through a *mouli*.

Meanwhile, cook the fish. Heat 1 tablespoon olive oil in a sauté pan. Cut the fish into large pieces and add these to the pan. Sauté over a gentle heat until cooked. Drain the pieces on paper towels, removing any visible bones, then put in a large bowl and shred finely with a fork. Stir the tomato sauce into the shredded fish, and beat until well mixed.

Finely chop the ham and green olives, then add them to the fish and tomato mixture, stirring until combined. Beat the eggs as for an omelet. Season lightly with salt and freshly ground black pepper, then beat into the fish mixture. Season to taste with paprika and cayenne, and salt and black pepper.

Grease a large bread pan with the rest of the oil. Pour the mixture into the pan and bake as in the previous recipe for 30 to 40 minutes, until cooked: The fish loaf will stay warm for up to 15 minutes in the pan outside the oven.

Meanwhile, prepare the peppers. Cut them in half lengthwise, remove the seeds and white cores, then char them under a hot broiler until the skins blister. Leave until they are cool enough to handle, then peel off the skins. Now slice them into even-size narrow strips.

Just before serving, unmold the loaf onto a dish. Arrange the strips of red pepper on top of the loaf and around it. Melt the butter in a small saucepan, squeeze in the lemon juice, and spoon it over the fish loaf and peppers; alternatively, coat with hollandaise. This dish can also be served cold with a light *rouille*, mayonnaise, or *anchoïade*.

Volailles et Viandes
Poultry, Game, and Meat

THE TIMES MAY be a-changing, but the meat course still remains the centerpiece of the French meal–the dish you just don't do without, even when time and appetite are limited.

The following selection is a very personal one. I give you recipes that have been with me for much of my life and that I am always happy to cook. Pot roasts and stews tend to steal the show, perhaps because, when I close my eyes and think of a kitchen, sooner or later a large black cast-iron *cocotte* materializes. It never goes away. The *cocotte* is the crucible of the French kitchen, well tempered and endlessly accommodating. I could go on happily about the miracles it performs, but a great deal has already been written, and very well too, on the romance of the *cocotte*, so I won't dwell on it. Do go and buy one, though, or get to know yours, if you have one already. You will not regret it.

Meat is an expensive commodity, even more so if it turns out a culinary disappointment. For this reason I only buy packed supermarket meat and poultry if I have to. There is no pleasure in it. I feel very strongly that the buying of meat should be a personal transaction. As a child or teenager, when I was dispatched on a shopping expedition, I was generally trusted to return with more or less the right groceries, vegetables, and fruit. Cheeses I was instructed to buy from one known shop, with the help of one particular assistant. But when it came to meat, my role was that of humble courier. The deal had always been discussed on the phone first, by my grandmother or my mother. The day's requirements had been carefully explained and the previous purchase commented on.

Whenever I go to a butcher's in France, I always feel that the standing in line is endless. The butchers and their customers seem to chat forever. It takes a while to readjust to the fact that nobody wants to rush the occasion. Buying meat is an important purchase that takes up a lot of the family's food budget. It needs to be given due consideration. Fortunately, things being what they are, standing in line at the butcher's is also a nice social occasion, time for a little moan and a good gossip.

Chaudfroid de Poulet
Chicken Chaudfroid

A GOOD PARTY dish, particularly popular, if my memory serves me right, with elderly members of the family. It is a great showcase for one of my favorite herbs, tarragon, sadly neglected outside France.

2 large chickens	Serves 8 to 10	sea salt
2 carrots		freshly ground black pepper
2 turnips		4 tablespoons (60 g) butter
2 leeks		4 tablespoons (60 g) flour
1 onion		1¼ cups (300 ml) *crème fraîche*
several sprigs of parsley and		or heavy cream
tarragon, plus extra tarragon	3 cloves	4 egg yolks
to finish the dish	1 cup (250 ml) white wine	1 or 2 lemons

THE DAY BEFORE YOU INTEND TO SERVE the dish, place the chickens side by side in a very large, heavy-bottomed saucepan. Peel, wash, and coarsely chop the carrots, turnips, leeks, and onion. Add to the pan with the parsley, tarragon, and cloves. Pour in the wine, and enough cold water to cover the chickens and vegetables.

Bring gently to a boil, skimming off any scum that comes up to the surface; season lightly with salt and freshly ground black pepper. Simmer for 45 to 60 minutes over a very moderate heat, until the chickens are cooked through. Leave them in the liquid until cool enough to handle, then lift the chickens out of the pot, drain well, and remove the skins. Leave the birds to get cold before jointing them as neatly as possible.

Meanwhile, vigorously boil the stock for 45 to 60 minutes until reduced by a third. Leave to cool. Carefully strain the stock into a saucepan through a strainer lined with cheesecloth or fine cloth; reserve.

To make the sauce, bring the reserved stock to a simmer; take off the heat. Melt the butter in another saucepan. Add the flour and cook for a couple of minutes, stirring vigorously to make a light roux. Pour in the hot chicken stock gradually, then bring to a boil, still stirring vigorously. Reduce the heat and simmer for about 10 minutes, stirring occasionally.

Remove the pan from the heat and leave to cool a little. Stir the cream into the sauce. Beat the egg yolks, and squeeze the lemon or lemons. Beat a couple of spoonfuls of the hot sauce into the egg yolks, then stir the mixture into the sauce, and continue stirring for a while. Season to taste with lemon juice, salt, and freshly ground black pepper.

Pat the chicken pieces dry with paper towels and arrange them on a large serving dish. Using a ladle, coat the chicken evenly with the sauce. Chill the dish overnight and just before serving, sprinkle with the remaining tarragon leaves.

LA POULE AU POT FARCIE
Stuffed Boiled Chicken

A GREAT ONE-POT DISH. All it takes is a little patience as the chicken must be allowed to simmer extremely slowly indeed. If giblets aren't available, use 1 slice each of cured ham and smoked bacon, or garlic mayonnaise, or *pistou* sauce.

1 large chicken, with its giblets for the stuffing (if available)	Serves 6	3⅓ cups (200 g) breadcrumbs made from day-old bread
¼ Savoy or white cabbage		2 cloves of garlic
sea salt		several sprigs of parsley
1 pound (450 g) carrots		2 eggs
14 ounces (400 g) turnips		sea salt
10 small to medium leeks		freshly ground black pepper
1 head of celery		
several sprigs of parsley and thyme	FOR THE STUFFING	TO SERVE
2 bay leaves	8 ounces (225 g) thickly cut smoked bacon	gherkins
freshly ground black pepper	7 ounces (200 g) cooked ham	mustard
		coarse kosher salt

PREPARE THE STUFFING. COMBINE THE liver, heart, and gizzard with the bacon, ham, breadcrumbs, garlic, and parsley in a food processor. Add the eggs to the bowl and process briefly. Season lightly with salt and more generously with freshly ground black pepper. Spoon the stuffing into the chicken's cavity. Sew up the cavity with a trussing needle and fine string, then truss the chicken with string.

Put the chicken in a very large, heavy-bottomed saucepan or Dutch oven. Cover with cold water and very gently bring to a boil over a low heat, skimming the surface as and when necessary.

Prepare the vegetables while the bird is coming to a boil. Blanch the cabbage for a few minutes in lightly salted boiling water. Peel the carrots and turnips. Carefully wash and trim the leeks and celery. Tie all the vegetables together in bundles.

After the chicken has simmered for 30 minutes, add the vegetables to the pot. Season with salt. Bring back to a low boil, and simmer for 1½ hours, skimming whenever necessary.

Just before serving, remove the chicken from the pot. Discard the strings and remove the stuffing from the bird, then cut the stuffing into pieces (it may fall apart a little). Serve the chicken in a large dish surrounded by the vegetables and stuffing. Strain the cooking liquid through a strainer, lined with cheesecloth or a fine cloth. Check the seasoning and use a little strained liquid to moisten the bird and vegetables. Transfer the rest to a sauceboat. Serve with gherkins, mustard, and coarse sea salt.

POULET AU VINAIGRE
Chicken with a Vinegar Sauce

ALONG WITH *FLIC*, *POULET* is one of the many words the French use to refer to a member of their police force. Moviemaker Claude Chabrol called one of his enjoyable piquant thrillers *Poulet au Vinaigre*—which somebody cleverly rendered into English as *Cop au Viu*, very passable menu French, if you ask me. I have wondered ever since if Monsieur Chabrol, a gourmet of great repute, had any strong views on the dish. This is not his recipe.

Serves 4 to 6

1 large chicken
2 tablespoons (30 ml) olive oil
1 tablespoon (15 g) butter
2 cloves of garlic
sea salt
freshly ground black pepper
1 tablespoon (15 ml) Dijon
    mustard
1 tablespoon (15 ml) tomato
    paste (purée)
3 tablespoons (45 ml) dry white
    wine
4 tablespoons (60 ml) good-
    quality white wine vinegar
3 tablespoons (45 ml) heavy
    cream

JOINT THE CHICKEN. HEAT THE OIL AND butter in a large sauté pan. Cut the cloves of garlic in half. Put the jointed chicken in the pan with the garlic and sauté for several minutes, turning the pieces over to color lightly and evenly. Season sparsely with salt and freshly ground black pepper, cover, and cook gently for 20 to 30 minutes, until the chicken pieces are cooked through; keep the heat low and shake the pan several times during the cooking.

Meanwhile, mix together in a bowl the mustard, tomato paste, and white wine. When the chicken is cooked, sprinkle the vinegar into the pan; stir for a few minutes until the liquid has reduced. Cover and leave over a low heat.

Remove the chicken from the pan and keep warm. Add the mustard mixture to the pan, turn up the heat a little, and stir for a couple of minutes. Spoon in the cream and heat through gently, stirring occasionally. Pour the sauce over the chicken and serve immediately.

COQ AU VIN
Chicken Cooked in Red Wine

I LOVE COOKING casseroles on top of the stove, lifting the lid, nosing the mixture, and giving it an encouraging stir or two, as it melts and blends into a rich, comforting dish. *Coq au vin* is one of my favorites. I find it so enjoyable to rediscover that I never quite cook it exactly the same way. The addition of chocolate to the ingredients is a recent one, inspired by South American cooking and–closer to home–reading Raymonde Charlon, formerly of *La Godille* in Brittany. Madame Charlon's little trick does add a distinct *je ne sais quoi* to the old classic.

Serves 6

1 large chicken
2 tablespoons (30 ml) oil
2 tablespoons (30 g) butter, plus extra to finish the sauce
4 ounces (120 g) thickly cut smoked bacon
1 large white Spanish onion
2 shallots

6 tablespoons (90 ml) brandy
1 tablespoon (15 g) flour
2½ cups (600 ml) Burgundy red wine
2 cloves of garlic
8 ounces (225 g) button mushrooms

1 ounce (30 g) bittersweet chocolate
a few sprigs each of parsley and thyme
2 bay leaves
sea salt
freshly ground black pepper

JOINT THE CHICKEN. HEAT THE OIL AND butter in a large Dutch oven or heavy-bottomed saucepan. Chop the bacon, onion, and shallots and sauté in the hot oil until lightly colored. Push to the side and add the chicken pieces. Sauté the chicken until golden, turning the pieces over to color evenly.

As soon as the chicken is a nice golden color, pour in the brandy and set alight. Once the flames have died down, sprinkle in flour and stir well with a wooden spoon. Pour in the wine. Finely chop the garlic, slice the mushrooms, and roughly grate the chocolate. Add them to the chicken with the sprigs of herbs and the bay leaves; stir well.

Turn up the heat and bring to a fast simmer, then cover and reduce the heat to moderately low. Cook for a good 30 minutes or until the chicken pieces are cooked, shaking the pan occasionally. Season to taste with salt and freshly ground black pepper. This dish tastes even better reheated and will benefit from being made in the morning–or even one day ahead. Reheat very gently, adding a little water if necessary–but not too much.

Remove the chicken pieces with tongs and put them on a plate; keep warm, and discard the sprigs of herbs and bay leaves.

Turn up the heat and reduce the sauce if it looks too thin, scraping the bottom of the Dutch oven with a wooden spoon or spatula. Stir in a good knob of butter, then return the chicken to the casserole and serve at once.

POULARDE À LA TOURANGELLE
Chicken Cooked in a Wine and Cream Sauce

A DELICATE *FRICASSÉE* FROM THE LOIRE, where it is often made with guinea fowl and Vouvray rather than just chicken and white wine. For me, this dish typifies the cooking of the area–fragrant, unpretentious, and making the most of the excellent local produce.

1 chicken or guinea fowl, without giblets	Serves 4	sea salt
1 tablespoon (15 ml) oil		freshly ground black pepper
3 tablespoons (45 g) butter		½ cup (120 ml) Vouvray or medium-dry white wine
1 onion		6 tablespoons (90 ml) light cream
2 slices of thickly cut bacon		1 lemon
1 clove of garlic		2 small egg yolks
5 ounces (150 g) button mushrooms	several sprigs each of thyme, parsley, and chives	

JOINT THE BIRD AND SOAK THE PIECES FOR a couple of hours in water at room temperature. Drain well and pat dry firmly with a clean cloth or paper towels.

In a sauté pan, heat the oil and butter. Chop the onion and bacon. Sauté in the pan for a few minutes over a gentle heat, then push to the sides and add the chicken pieces. Sauté until they are lightly colored all over.

Meanwhile, crush the garlic and slice the mushrooms. Add to the pan with the fresh herbs. Season lightly with salt and freshly ground black pepper. Moisten with the white wine, then partly cover the pan and cook over a low heat until the chicken is cooked and the liquid well reduced; this takes about 20 to 30 minutes.

Pour the cream into the pan and stir until it is heated through, then remove the chicken from the pan with tongs or a draining spoon; keep warm on a serving dish. Squeeze the lemon and mix the juice with the egg yolks. Away from the heat, stir this mixture into the pan. Check the seasoning and spoon the sauce over the chicken. Serve immediately.

POULET CHASSEUR
Huntsman's Chicken

WHEN I FIRST ate *poulet chasseur*, I was also at the time endlessly listening to the first record I ever owned, *Peter and the Wolf*, narrated by Gérard Philipe (taking time off from *Fanfan La Tulipe*). So the dish stayed linked in my mind with the sound of horns and the picture of three very Russian huntsmen stalking through a forest. By the time I came across *pollo cacciatore* years later and opened my pocket Italian dictionary, I was ready to enjoy the fact that huntsmen and country dishes, like fairy tales, have much in common the world over.

4 chicken leg portions
1 tablespoon (15 ml) oil
2 tablespoons (30 g) butter,
   plus extra to finish
3 shallots
1 clove of garlic
1 level tablespoon (15 g) flour

Serves 4

3 tablespoons (45 ml) brandy
6 tablespoons (90 ml) dry white
   wine
chicken stock or water

sea salt
freshly ground black pepper
2 tomatoes
4 ounces (120 g) cremini
   (brown cap) mushrooms
several sprigs of chervil and
   tarragon

HEAT THE OIL AND BUTTER. FINELY CHOP the shallots and garlic. Sauté the chicken pieces in the hot fat with the shallots and garlic, turning the pieces over to color evenly.

Sprinkle the chicken pieces with the flour. Add the brandy, then the white wine and enough chicken stock or water to just cover the chicken; stir well. Season with salt and freshly ground black pepper, cover, and simmer over a moderate heat for 20 to 30 minutes; shake the pan occasionally during cooking.

Meanwhile, blanch, skin, seed, and roughly chop the tomatoes, then slice the mushrooms. Stir the tomatoes and mushrooms into the pan. Cover and simmer for 10 minutes, or until the chicken is cooked through. Remove the chicken from the pan and arrange on a serving dish; keep warm while you finish off the sauce.

Turn up the heat to reduce the sauce. Snip the chervil and tarragon into the pan, and stir well for a minute or two, then swirl in a good knob of butter. Check the seasoning and pour the sauce over the chicken pieces. Serve immediately.

PETIT CONFIT DE CANARD
Quick Duck Confit

THE FRENCH "COLONY" IN LONDON is large and thriving. For a few years now I have been hosting cookery sessions for an enthusiastic group of expatriate French women known as Le Cooking Club de Londres Accueil. The idea is that I demonstrate four or five dishes, and then produce lunch with the help of my friend Marie-Laure. I end up hoarse-voiced after talking over the noise generated by an audience of a dozen *bavardes* torn between discussing new recipe ideas and catching up on gossip. My guinea pigs are frank and vocal about which of my dishes pass the test. They also generously contribute to my stock of recipes. This one is Brigitte Castaing's deliciously easy and light take on duck confit. I have also cooked it successfully with rabbit and free-range chicken (use large birds and reduce the cooking time by 30 minutes if cooking drumsticks rather than leg portions).

Serves 4 to 6

3 heaping tablespoons (50 g) coarse kosher salt several sprigs thyme, chopped	2 teaspoons (10 g) Chinese five-spice powder 6 duck leg portions	about 1¾ pints (1 liter) sunflower oil or mild-flavored olive oil freshly ground black pepper

IN A BOWL, MIX THE SALT, CHOPPED thyme, and five-spice powder. Using a sharp knife, make a few small slits through the duck skin into the flesh. Rub the duck with the seasoned salt, pressing well. Cover and chill for at least 2 hours, or up to 24 hours if convenient.

Rinse the duck under cold running water. Drain and pat dry with a clean towel. Cut off any loose bits of skin.

Heat the oven to 275°F. Put the duck in a deep ovenproof pot just large enough to take the pieces side by side. Pour in the oil–you should have about 2 inches (5 cm) of oil on top of the duck. The exact amount of oil you need depends on the pot you use–make sure there is a clear 2 inches (5 cm) between the surface of the oil and the rim of the pot. Put in the oven and cook uncovered for 2½ hours, turning the pieces over once after about 1½ hours.

Lift the pieces from the oil and drain well, then place on a clean towel or a thick layer of paper towels. Pat to get rid of excess oil. Season generously with black pepper. Serve as soon as possible with *gratin dauphinois* (see page 122) or *pommes de terre sautées Tata Baucher* (see page 124).

The confit freezes well and can be reheated with 1 tablespoon of the oil used for cooking in a large skillet. Once drained through a strainer, the rest of the oil can be used again for frying potatoes and cooking another confit.

PERDREAUX EN CASSEROLE
Pot-Roasted Partridges

A RECIPE FROM MY MOTHER. The sauce is best finished off with slightly bitter orange juice. So, if Sevilles aren't in season, taste it and, if it seems on the sweet side, add a dash of lemon or grapefruit juice.

Serves 4

4 tablespoons (60 g) butter
2 oven-ready partridges
a few sprigs of parsley and
   thyme
1 bay leaf
1 heaping tablespoon (20 g)
   flour

1 cup (250 ml) white wine
sea salt
freshly ground black pepper
cayenne pepper
4 ounces (120 g) cured ham,
   thinly cut
2 Seville oranges, or 1 large
   juicy orange

ORANGES DE BLANCHARD

HEAT THE BUTTER IN A DUTCH OVEN. Over a moderate heat, sauté the partridges until brown on all sides. Remove them from the pan with a draining spoon, allowing the juices to drip back into the pan; reserve the partridges. Carefully snip the parsley, thyme, and bay leaf.

Sprinkle the flour into the pan and stir until slightly colored, then pour in the white wine and add the herbs. Season with very little salt and freshly ground black pepper and a small pinch of cayenne. Cook, stirring vigorously, until the liquid begins to bubble. Reduce the heat a little and simmer for a good 5 minutes, stirring occasionally. Return the partridges to the pan, cover, and simmer very gently over a low heat for about 20 minutes.

Meanwhile, chop the ham into small pieces. Squeeze the juice from the orange or oranges into a bowl.

Transfer the partridges onto a hot serving dish. Add the ham and orange juice to the pan, stir until heated through, scraping up the sediments from the bottom of the pan. Pour the sauce over the partridges. Serve immediately.

MAGRETS DE CANARD À L'ORANGE
Duck Breasts with Orange

CANARD À L'ORANGE had become such a tired cliché by the early 1980s that we all heaved a sigh of relief when it was knocked off the menu by very rare *magrets* dramatically arranged on a bed of red fruit sauce. Now that these too have palled, may I suggest these duck breasts with orange? They are quick to cook, quicker still if, unlike me, you prefer them very pink. The little orange, lemon, and Cointreau sauce is adapted from my mother's much sweeter original recipe.

Serves 4

2 large, boned duck breasts,
   each weighing about
   12 ounces (350 g)
sea salt
freshly ground black pepper
2 oranges
1 lemon
1 scant teaspoon (5 g)
   cornstarch (cornflour)
1 ounce (30 g) chilled unsalted
   butter, diced
4 tablespoons (60 ml)
   Cointreau

WITH A SMALL AND VERY SHARP KNIFE, score the skin side of the duck breasts—deeply enough to cut into the flesh—several times in long parallel lines. Season with salt and freshly ground black pepper. Heat a heavy-bottomed skillet until hot. Put the breasts in the pan skin side down. There is enough fat in the skin not to need any more fat. Cook for a good 10 to 15 minutes over a moderate heat.

Meanwhile, peel one of the oranges and the lemon. Chop the zests very finely and blanch for a couple of minutes in a little boiling water; drain well. Squeeze the oranges and lemon.

After about 10 minutes, discard any excess fat, and turn over the duck breasts. Lower the heat and cook them for 3 to 5 minutes on the flesh side—the timing will depend on how well cooked you like your duck. Remove the breasts from the pan and set aside to relax, keeping them hot on a heated serving dish under a heated plate.

Stir in the cornstarch and butter, then add the orange and lemon juices, and the drained, finely chopped zest. Stir for a couple of minutes over a moderate heat, until simmering. Add the Cointreau and season with a little salt and more generously with freshly ground black pepper. Spoon or pour the sauce over the duck breasts and serve immediately.

CARNARD AUX PÊCHES
Roast Duck with Peaches

My father's recipe, and very good and mellow it is, too. Peaches canned in juice are worth looking for, otherwise rinse the peaches quickly under the faucet (after draining off the syrup) to get rid of the excess sweetness. If fresh peaches are available, peel (see page 138) and use them.

4- to 5-pound (1.8- to 2.3-kg) oven-ready duck	Serves 4	1 large can white peaches, drained and halved
sea salt		3 tablespoons (45 ml) heavy cream
freshly ground black pepper		3 tablespoons (45 ml) brandy

Heat the oven to 350°F. Rinse the duck well inside and out and pat dry with a paper towel. Score the skin with the point of a sharp knife. Season well inside and out with salt and freshly ground black pepper.

Stuff the cavity through the tail end with the cream and some of the peaches, reserving the rest. Put the duck on a rack in a roasting pan, and roast in the oven for 1½ hours. After half an hour, prick the skin, baste the duck with the cooking juices and add the rest of the peaches to the roasting pan. Baste the duck again occasionally.

When the duck is cooked through, lift the rack off the roasting pan. Arrange the peaches from the roasting pan on a serving dish; discard much of the fat. Spoon the stuffing out of the cavity into the roasting pan. Add the duck and the peaches used in the stuffing to the serving dish. Place the pan over a moderate heat and pour in the brandy. Stir the mixture for 2 minutes, scraping the bottom of the pan. Strain the sauce into a sauceboat, season, and serve.

CANARD AUX OLIVES
Duck with Olives

I sometimes use the same method for chicken and serve it with rice and mushrooms.

4- to 5-pound (1.8- to 2.3-kg) oven-ready duck	Serves 4	1 few sprigs of thyme
sea salt		1 bay leaf
freshly ground black pepper		1 large white Spanish onion
1 tablespoon (15 ml) oil	1¼ cups (300 ml) dry white wine	2 large tomatoes
2 tablespoons (30 g) butter		1½ cups (225 g) pitted green olives

Rinse and season the duck as above. In a large, Dutch oven, heat the oil and butter. Sauté the duck in the hot fat until the skin is crisp and golden on all sides.

Spoon a couple of tablespoons of hot fat into a skillet and discard the rest. Add the wine and herbs, cover, and reduce the heat. Cook for 30 minutes, basting twice.

Meanwhile, chop the onion and tomatoes and sauté in the reserved duck fat over a low heat until soft, stirring occasionally. Stir the onion and tomato mixture into the pot, then cover and simmer for 30 minutes more.

Stir in the olives, and a little water if the mixture looks too dry. Cover and simmer for another 30 minutes. Serve very hot.

CANARD AUX NAVETS
Braised Duck with Turnips

I DON'T KNOW where the marriage of duck and turnips was made, but it is certainly a happy one. Having tried a number of approaches to the dish, I now think that dividing the turnips between the pot and the skillet produces the best results, even if it is slightly more fiddly. If you don't like turnips, replace them with fleshy fat mushrooms, parsnips (not at all French, but never mind), or baby onions.

4- to 5-pound (1.8- to 2.3-kg)
  oven-ready duck
sea salt
freshly ground black pepper
2¼ pounds (1 kg) baby turnips
1 tablespoon (15 ml) oil
2 tablespoons (30 g) butter,
  plus extra to finish the sauce

Serves 4 or 5

1 cup (250 ml) chicken or
  vegetable stock
2 or 3 teaspoons (10 or 15 g)
  sugar
4 tablespoons (60 ml) white
  wine

RINSE THE DUCK WELL INSIDE AND OUT, and pat dry with paper towels. Season well inside and out with salt and freshly ground black pepper. Peel the turnips and cut them neatly into halves or quarters, depending on size. Reserve 8 to 10 pieces and cook the rest of the turnips in lightly salted boiling water for 5 to 10 minutes.

Meanwhile, in a large, Dutch oven or heavy-bottomed saucepan, heat the oil and butter. Sauté the duck in the hot fat until lightly golden on all sides. Pour out the fat into a skillet to use for browning the turnips. Add the stock and the reserved turnips to the pan with the duck. Cover tightly and cook over a low heat for about 1½ hours.

Drain the first batch of turnips and set aside. When the duck is nearly cooked, heat the fat in the skillet and add the turnips. Sprinkle them with the sugar and sauté gently for 15 to 20 minutes over a low heat, shaking the pan occasionally and turning the turnips over.

Remove the duck from its pan and arrange it and the sautéed turnips on a serving dish; keep this dish warm. Turn up the heat, add the white wine to the duck stock, and let the cooking liquid reduce a little, stirring well and mashing the turnips roughly with the back of a wooden spoon. Season with salt and freshly ground black pepper. Strain some of the sauce over the duck and the rest into a bowl or sauceboat, discarding the remaining mashed turnips. Stir a little butter into the sauceboat to finish and serve hot with the duck and turnips.

Faisan Rôti Farci
Stuffed Roast Pheasant

Like millions of other Frenchmen, my father used to go shooting regularly on a Sunday, so pheasant often featured on our menu during the autumn and winter months. Far too often it seemed, to his daughters, because we much preferred chicken and said so loudly every time its elegant relative appeared on the table. In the end my mother gave up setting pearls in front of her piglets and served pheasant to her dinner party guests instead.

1 plump pheasant, dressed, gizzards reserved
4 thin slices unsmoked bacon
1 extremely small jar or can of truffle parings
3 tablespoons (45 ml) brandy

Serves 2 to 4

1 tablespoon (15 g) breadcrumbs made from day-old bread
5 tablespoons (75 g) butter
sea salt
freshly ground black pepper
4 thick pieces of bread

Heat the oven to 425°F. Prepare the stuffing. Rinse the gizzards, and process them quickly with 1 slice of bacon, the truffle parings and their juice, 1 tablespoon of brandy, the breadcrumbs, and a good knob of butter in a food processor. Season with a little salt and freshly ground black pepper. Rinse the cavity of the pheasant and pat it dry with paper towels. Spoon the stuffing into the cavity, then sew it up, using a trussing needle and fine string.

Stretch the remaining bacon slices with the help of a rolling pin or metal spatula. Wrap the bird well in the bacon and tie with string.

Toast the bread very lightly. Melt the rest of the butter in a small saucepan. Lay the toasted bread pieces on the bottom of a roasting pan. Stand a rack in the pan and place the pheasant on the rack. Trickle a little melted butter over the pheasant. Keep the melted butter warm.

Roast the pheasant in the oven for about 50 minutes, occasionally dribbling more melted butter over it. If the bread looks as if it is about to burn, remove it from the pan and reserve in a warm place. Remove the bacon larding and discard with the strings, or reserve the bacon for a salad. Add the rest of the brandy to the melted butter. Return the bread to the pan, if necessary. Dribble the butter and brandy over the pheasant, season lightly with salt and freshly ground black pepper, and return to the oven for 5 to 10 minutes more, until golden brown.

To serve, cut off and discard the string. Extract the stuffing and divide it between the pieces of buttery toast. Arrange the toast, stuffing, and pheasant on a dish. Serve hot.

Terrine de Faisan

Pheasant Terrine

La terrine maison. We tended to help ourselves from the dish, not terribly elegantly, and served bread, butter, and gherkins with this. For special occasions, however, this terrine looks most presentable, unmolded onto a gleaming platter, cut into thin overlapping slices, and surrounded by a small border of chopped aspic and a tiny bouquet of parsley.

Serves 8

1 plump pheasant
18 ounces (500 g) lean pork
   sparerib meat
a few sprigs of thyme
3 sage leaves
1 bay leaf
3 cloves of garlic
sea salt
freshly ground black pepper

6 tablespoons (90 ml) brandy
   or marc
2 large eggs
6 thin slices of smoked bacon

For the aspic:
2 carrots
several sprigs of thyme,
   parsley, and chervil

1 bay leaf
6 black peppercorns
1¼ cups (300 ml) dry white
   wine
1 heaping tablespoon (30 g)
   good unflavored aspic
   powder
2 teaspoons (10 ml) brandy
2 tablespoons (30 ml) Madeira
   wine

Heat the oven to 325°F. Joint and bone the pheasant. Reserve the breast fillets, and also set aside the bones. Bone and trim the pork, again reserving the bones.

Finely grind, or quickly whizz together in a food processor, the pheasant meat, including the liver, the pork, thyme, sage, and bay leaves, and the garlic. Season the meat mixture with salt and more generously with freshly ground black pepper. Stir in the brandy and the eggs and work the mixture well, preferably with your hands.

Stretch the bacon slices with the help of a rolling pin or metal spatula. Line a terrine dish (or a bread pan) with a couple of bacon slices, then spread in an even layer of meat and egg mixture. Cut the breast fillets into neat long strips, and place 2 or 3 strips over the meat and egg layer. Cover with another layer of breast fillets on top. Spread in another layer of meat mixture, then cover with bacon rashers. Cover the dish tightly.

Line a large roasting pan with a thick layer of newspapers. Place the dish in the middle of the pan. Pour in boiling water to come halfway up the sides of the dish. Carefully put the pan in the oven and bake for a good 3 hours, pouring in more boiling water as and when necessary to keep the halfway level.

While the terrine is in the oven, prepare the aspic. Peel the carrots. Put the reserved bones in a large saucepan with the peeled carrots, the sprigs of herbs, the bay leaf, and the peppercorns. Cover with the white wine and 3¾ cups (850 ml) cold water. Slowly bring to a boil, skimming off any greasy scum that comes up to the surface. Partly cover and simmer for a couple of hours, skimming off occasionally. Turn up the heat toward the end–you should end up with 2½ cups (600 ml) stock. Strain through a strainer lined with cheesecloth, or through a *chinois*, into a bowl. Stand in cold water to cool.

Leave the terrine to relax in the oven for 15 minutes after you turn off the heat. Remove from the oven, take off the cover, and leave for a few minutes. Meanwhile, transfer the stock to a saucepan, and make the aspic following the package instructions. Stir in the brandy and Madeira wine.

Remove the bacon slices from the top of the terrine. Pierce the meat deeply in several places with a skewer. Pour the warm aspic liquid over the meat. Leave to cool and refrigerate overnight.

LAPIN EN DAUBE
Pot-Roasted Rabbit

A USEFUL DISH that slowly cooks all by itself. I have been vaguer than usual about the timing, since it will depend entirely on the age and provenance of your rabbit. If you prefer, follow exactly the same method, but use hare, kid, or chicken.

Serves 4

1 rabbit, jointed, or 4 to 6
  rabbit pieces
6 thickly cut slices smoked
  bacon
1 large white Spanish onion
1 carrot
several sprigs each of parsley,
  thyme, and rosemary
2 bay leaves
3 juniper berries
2 cloves of garlic
sea salt
freshly ground black pepper
⅔ cup (150 ml) dry white wine

HEAT THE OVEN TO 300°F. FLATTEN AND stretch the slices of bacon with the help of a rolling pin—I wrap my old wooden one in plastic wrap first in the interests of hygiene. Line the bottom of a medium-size Dutch oven with 3 slices and reserve the rest.

Slice the onion and carrot and arrange the slices on the bacon. Snip half the herbs over the vegetables and add the rabbit pieces, then the bay leaves and juniper berries. Crush the garlic and put on top of the rabbit pieces. Snip in the rest of the herbs. Season with a little salt and more generously with freshly ground black pepper. Moisten with the wine. Cover with the rest of the bacon slices. Cover the dish and cook in the oven for 2 to 3 hours, until the rabbit is very tender. Serve piping hot.

Lapin à la Moutarde
Rabbit with Mustard

I still love mustard and am known to use it surreptitiously with roast chicken or lamb, but over the years, my *lapin à la moutarde* has become gradually milder. The recipe below is the state of the art at the moment. In the old days, I stirred in an extra couple of tablespoons of milder mustard before adding the liquid to the browned and floured rabbit. Try it both ways and also experiment with different mustards until you get the results you like best.

Serves 4

1 rabbit, jointed, or 4 to 6
  rabbit pieces
1 tablespoon (15 ml) oil
3 tablespoons (45 g) butter,
  plus extra to finish
sea salt
freshly ground black pepper

1 tablespoon (15 g) flour
1 clove of garlic
2 shallots
a few sprigs each of thyme and
  rosemary
7 ounces (200 ml) chicken
  stock or white wine, plus
  extra liquid if needed

3 tablespoons (45 ml) brandy
3 tablespoons (45 ml) strong
  Dijon mustard, or your
  favorite mustard
½ cup (120 ml) light cream
a few sprigs of parsley, to finish

Heat the oil and butter in a Dutch oven or sauté pan. Add the rabbit pieces to the pan, season with salt and freshly ground black pepper, and sprinkle in the flour. Sauté for a few minutes, turning the pieces over regularly. Crush the garlic and finely chop the shallots. Add to the pan. Snip in the thyme and rosemary.

Moisten with the chicken stock or white wine, stir, and cook, covered, over a low heat for about 45 minutes—the exact timing will depend on the rabbit you are using. Shake the pan occasionally and reduce the heat if necessary—rabbit pieces tend to shred and stick all too easily to the bottom of pans. Moisten with a little extra liquid if needed. Heat the brandy and pour it over the rabbit. Set alight, then remove the rabbit pieces from the pan and keep them warm on a plate or serving dish while you finish the sauce.

Remove the sprigs of thyme and rosemary. Stir in the mustard and the cream. Heat for a couple of minutes, still stirring.

Snip in the parsley and swirl in a good-size knob of butter, then pour the sauce over the rabbit. If you prefer to serve the rabbit from the pan, gently stir the pieces into the sauce instead.

LAPIN À LA BIÈRE ET AUX PRUNEAUX
Rabbit with Ale and Prunes

HAVING ONCE OVERHEARD grown-ups exchanging dire tales of myxomatosis, and not realizing that they were reminiscing and that the big epidemic was a thing of the past, I spent my childhood carefully avoiding rabbits, both in the hutch and on the plate. What a good thing I missed out on! This recipe converted me in the end. If you share my early phobia, don't give up on this rich, dark dish. For rabbit read pork, or stewing steak. The recipe is excellent for cheaper cuts of beef; trim off as much visible fat as possible, and double the cooking time.

1 rabbit, about 1¾ pounds
  (800 g), cut into 4 to 6 pieces
flour for coating
2 tablespoons (30 ml) oil
8 ounces (225 g) thickly cut
  smoked bacon
1 onion
several sprigs of thyme

Serves 4

2 bay leaves
2½ cups (600 ml) brown ale
6 ounces (175 g) moist pitted
  prunes
2 tablespoons (30 ml) wine
  vinegar

sea salt
freshly ground black pepper

TO SERVE
1 large slice *pain de campagne*
  or mixed-grain toast
Dijon mustard

COAT THE RABBIT PIECES LIGHTLY WITH flour. Heat the oil in a heavy-bottomed Dutch oven or large saucepan. Add the rabbit pieces and gently sauté until golden, turning them over to brown evenly.

Cut the bacon into small 1-inch (2.5-cm) pieces and chop the onion. Add bacon and onion to the sautéed rabbit pieces with the thyme and bay leaves. Sprinkle with a little flour and stir well, then pour in the ale.

Partly cover the casserole and cook for about 40 minutes over a low heat. Add the prunes and wine vinegar, give a good stir, and continue to cook for 20 minutes. Again, leave the lid only partly covering the pot.

Taste and season the sauce. Generously spread Dijon mustard over both sides of the piece of toast and add to the casserole. Cover completely and cook for 10 minutes more before serving.

Civet de Lièvre
Jugged Hare

To make a proper jugged hare, you need to collect the blood as you skin and gut the animal. This you use to make a liaison, which enriches and finishes off this "noble dish." You also need "your two best bottles of red wine." The incomparable Edouard de Pomiane, whose words I am humbly borrowing, had only one regret–that he was not wealthy enough to "make a *civet* with Chambertin" . . . . Back in Touraine, we used Bourgueil, one bottle to cook with and one (or two) to drink with the dish.

If you aren't able to get hold of a whole hare, complete with blood, use a little *beurre manié* made by mashing together flour and butter (see page 12) to thicken the sauce. And if you can't find a hare, use rabbit instead. The marinade does wonders for even the toughest of bunnies. It won't be quite the real thing, but it will still be a marvelous casserole.

This dish is traditionally served with croutons.

	Serves 6	
1 hare		3 tablespoons (45 g) butter
1 bottle of good red wine		1 tablespoon (15 g) flour
4 tablespoons (60 ml) brandy	3 bay leaves	sea salt
2 cloves of garlic	6 black peppercorns	freshly ground black pepper
1 large white Spanish onion	4 thickly cut slices of smoked	8 ounces (225 g) button
several sprigs each of thyme	bacon	mushrooms
and parsley	1 tablespoon (15 ml) oil	croutons, to serve, if liked

Carefully skin and gut the hare; collect all the blood you can into a bowl. Devein the liver if necessary, also cutting out any yellowish bits, and add it to the blood; cover and chill until needed. Joint the animal, cutting the back pieces with the help of your strongest knife and a mallet–or make a deal with your friendly local butcher.

Put the pieces of hare in a deep dish and cover with the wine and brandy. Finely chop the garlic and onion and snip the thyme and parsley, then add them all to the marinade, with the bay leaves and peppercorns. Marinate for 24 hours in a cool place.

A few hours before you intend to serve the hare, chop the bacon. Remove the hare from the marinade, drain well, and pat dry with a clean towel or paper towels; reserve the marinade.

Heat the oil and butter in a Dutch oven or large sauté pan. Put the chopped bacon in the pan and stir over a medium heat for a couple of minutes, then add the hare. Stir for 5 to 10 minutes until the meat begins to turn brown. Sprinkle in the flour and stir for a minute, then pour in the marinade. Season to taste, stir, cover, and cook over a low heat for at least 1 hour, perhaps 2–the meat is cooked when it begins to come off the bones easily.

Slice the mushrooms and stir them into the pan toward the end of cooking. Remove the reserved liver from the bowl, chop it very finely, and stir it into the pan. Simmer for a few more minutes.

Now finish the sauce. Spoon a little of the cooking liquid into the blood to warm it up. Away from the heat, stir it into the sauce until well blended, return to the heat, and simmer briskly for 1 minute, stirring all the time–the sauce should be a smooth, dark brown. If you reheat the dish, it will taste just as good though the sauce won't look quite as appealing since it tends to separate. Serve with croutons, if you like.

BLANQUETTE DE VEAU
Veal in a Cream and Mushroom Sauce

A CLASSIC OF BOURGEOIS COOKING, and quite rightly so. Delicate *blanquette* is a dish that does not like to be rushed. After years of producing not unpalatable concoctions that were the color of milky coffee—unkindly called *brunettes* by the family—I adopted a gentler and more patient approach and, lo, my *blanquettes* turned a grateful shade of white.
Cook *blanquettes* on a day you want to relax in your kitchen and serve it with good plain rice and a bowl of small gherkins.

2¾ pounds (1.2 kg) breast of veal	**Serves 6 to 8**	5 ounces (150 g) pearl onions
1 carrot		1½ large lemons
1 large white Spanish onion		5 ounces (150 g) pearl mushrooms
several sprigs each of thyme and parsley	1¼ cups (300 ml) dry white wine	3 tablespoons (45 g) butter
2 bay leaves	sea salt	2 level tablespoons (30 g) flour
	freshly ground black pepper	1 or 2 extra-large egg yolks
		½ cup (120 ml) *crème fraîche*

TRIM THE BREAST OF VEAL, DISCARDING fat and sinew as necessary, and cut into 1½-inch (4-cm) pieces. Soak overnight or for several hours in plenty of fresh cold water. Once the veal has had a good soaking, peel the carrot and cut it into 4 chunks. Quarter the onion. Put the herbs and bay leaves on a small piece of cheesecloth, make into a bag and tie with a string. Drain the veal.

Put the veal with the vegetables and cheesecloth bag in a large, heavy-bottomed saucepan. Pour in the wine and add just enough cold water to cover. Over a very moderate heat, bring slowly to a low boil. Conscientiously skim off any scum that may come up to the surface. Season lightly with salt and freshly ground black pepper. Reduce the heat a little and simmer *very gently* for 1¼ to 1½ hours, skimming whenever necessary. The meat should feel tender when you pierce it with a fork at the end of cooking.

Meanwhile, peel the pearl onions and blanch for 5 minutes in lightly salted water. Squeeze the lemons. Trim and slice the mushrooms, and blanch well in boiling water with a dash of lemon juice for a couple of minutes. Drain the onions and mushrooms.

Strain the stock out of the pan into a bowl or pitcher, leaving the veal in the pan. Discard the cheesecloth bag, then add the drained onions and mushrooms to the pan. Sprinkle with a little lemon juice and then cover to keep warm. If you want to cook the dish in stages, this is a good time to break off; allow a good 30 minutes to finish off later. And do make sure you reheat everything gently.

Melt the butter in a saucepan. Add the flour and stir for 1 minute to make a very pale roux—do not let it color. Pour the hot stock into the roux, and bring to a boil, stirring vigorously. Simmer gently for a good 10 to 15 minutes, stirring frequently, until the sauce is smooth and thickened. Now beat the egg yolk or yolks in a bowl, stir in a little hot sauce, then the *crème fraîche*, and beat until thoroughly combined. Pour the mixture into the saucepan and stir over a low heat; do not boil.

Pour the sauce over the veal and vegetables. Return to a low heat and stir carefully for a couple of minutes until heated through. Sprinkle in the rest of the lemon juice, check the seasoning, stir, and serve immediately.

Veau aux Girolles
Veal with Wild Mushrooms

MAKE THIS OLD-FASHIONED DISH with the best mushrooms you think you can afford. I must admit that I only use little yellow horn-shaped *girolles* (also called *chanterelles*) if I have been lucky enough to be able to gather my own. Otherwise, I use small brown ones. I only buy wild mushrooms to enjoy them on their own, fried in the pan with a little butter, a hint of garlic, and plenty of chopped parsley.

Serves 6

2¾ pounds (1.2 kg) tender veal
   from the shoulder or leg, tied
   to make a neat joint
4 baby carrots
4 shallots
2 cloves of garlic
3 tablespoons (45 ml) olive oil
4 tablespoons (60 g) butter,
   plus extra to finish
1 cup (250 ml) medium-sweet
   white wine
sea salt
freshly ground black pepper
1½ pounds (750 g) *girolles* or
   other fragrant mushrooms
2 tablespoons (30 g) fresh
   breadcrumbs
a few sprigs of parsley and
   chervil

WIPE AND SLICE THE CARROTS. FINELY chop the shallots and crush the garlic. Heat 1 tablespoon of oil and a good knob of butter in a Dutch oven or sauté pan. Sauté the carrots, shallots, and garlic for 1 minute over a very moderate heat, then add the veal joint and sauté until it looks even colored, turning it over gradually.

Moisten with half the wine and a similar amount of water. Season lightly with salt and freshly ground black pepper, then cover tightly.

Reduce the heat and cook very slowly for a good hour. Leave the meat to cool and relax a little. Heat the oven to 425°F.

Meanwhile, trim and wipe the mushrooms. Heat the rest of the oil in a large skillet with a knob of butter. Add the mushrooms and let them sweat for a few minutes over a moderate heat, frequently shaking the pan. Season them with salt and freshly ground black pepper, then drain on paper towels. Cut the veal into thin slices. Spread half the mushrooms in a gratin dish. Arrange the slices of veal on top of the mushrooms.

Pour the rest of the wine into the Dutch oven or sauté pan. Stir over a moderately high heat for a minute or two, scraping the bottom of the pan. Strain the pan juices over the veal. Cover with the rest of the mushrooms and sprinkle with the breadcrumbs. Snip the herbs over the breadcrumbs, then dot with the rest of the butter. Finish the dish in the oven for 5 minutes, until golden. Serve immediately.

CÔTES DE PORC AU CIDRE ET À L'OIGNON

Pan-Fried Pork Chops with Onion and Vinegar

A GOOD PAN-FRY to serve with sautéed apple slices, mashed potatoes, or *gratin dauphinois* (see page 122).

Serves 4

4 pork chops, not too lean and cut fairly thick
1 clove of garlic
a few sprigs of thyme
4 sage leaves
freshly ground black pepper
4 tablespoons (60 ml) medium-

dry cider or white wine
1 small onion
1 shallot
olive oil, if needed

3 tablespoons (45 ml) cider or white wine vinegar
3 tablespoons (45 ml) light cream
2 teaspoons (10 ml) mild Dijon mustard
sea salt

CUT THE GARLIC AND RUB THE CHOPS well with the cut sides of the garlic. Snip the thyme and sage leaves over the chops, then sprinkle with freshly ground black pepper; rub this seasoning well in on both sides. Cover with plastic wrap and set aside at room temperature for about 1 hour.

Slit the fat around the chops at 1-inch (2.5-cm) intervals. Heat a sauté pan and put the chops in the pan. Cook them over a moderately high heat on both sides for a few minutes, until they turn brown and some fat runs out, then reduce the heat, moisten with the wine or cider and the same amount of water. Cover and cook very gently for 15 to 20 minutes. Remove the chops from the pan with tongs or a pancake turner and keep them warm on a heated serving dish under a heated plate.

Meanwhile, chop the onion and shallot finely. If the chops haven't released much fat, add a little olive oil to the pan juices. Soften the onion and shallot for a few minutes over a moderate heat, stirring frequently. Add the vinegar, scrape the bottom of the pan well, and bring to a simmer. Stir in the cream and mustard until hot. Season to taste with salt and a little extra pepper and spoon the sauce over the chops. Serve immediately.

PORC À LA BOULANGÈRE
Roast Pork with Potatoes

A WEEKEND ROAST after my own heart. Any leftovers will be delicious served with a little garlicky mayonnaise. Use the same method with a leg or shoulder of lamb; it will work just as well.

Serves 6

2 pounds (900 g) waxy
    potatoes
1 large white Spanish onion
oil for greasing
a few sprigs each of parsley
    and thyme

sea salt
freshly ground black pepper
about 1¼ cups (300 ml) chicken
    stock (see page 12), light beef
    stock, or water

4 tablespoons (60 g) butter
3 pounds (1.5 kg) loin of pork,
    boned, trimmed, and tied
2 or 3 cloves of garlic
4 sage leaves

HEAT THE OVEN TO 325°F. PEEL AND slice the potatoes fairly thickly. Thinly slice the onion. Grease a large gratin dish. Spread the sliced potatoes and onion over the bottom of the dish. Snip in the fresh herbs and season lightly with salt and freshly ground black pepper. Pour in just enough stock or water to cover the vegetables. Dot generously with butter and cover with foil. Cook in the oven for about 1 hour.

Now prepare the loin of pork. Cut the garlic and sage leaves into slivers. Using the point of a small, sharp knife, make several deep slits into the pork fat and insert the slivers of garlic and sage well into the slits. Rub the loin of pork with a little salt and more generously with freshly ground black

pepper. Set aside at room temperature for about 40 minutes.

Very lightly grease the bottom of a sauté pan. Heat the pan and brown the pork lightly and evenly on all sides over a moderately high heat. Take the potatoes out of the oven, uncover, and place the pork on top of the potatoes, replacing the foil before returning to the oven. Turn up the heat to 375°F and cook for 1¼ to 1½ hours, until the pork is tender and cooked through; remove the foil for the last 15 minutes.

This dish is best served simply. Leave the pork to relax for a few minutes, then remove it from the potatoes, cut into thin slices and arrange the slices, overlapping slightly, back on top of the potatoes.

CASSOULET MAISON
Pork and Haricot Bean Casserole

THIS RECIPE IS RELAXED, less fatty than most–and likely to be frowned on by *cassoulet* purists, since I include tomatoes. As I understand it, *cassoulet* is a flexible feast. One ingredient that cannot be left out is the *confit* (available from good gourmet delicatessens) with its inimitable fat and filamentous texture. Best prepared a day or two ahead, *cassoulet* makes a splendid *pièce de résistance* for a winter party. Drink with Cahors or Fitou wine. Mop up the juices with good bread and follow with heaps of sharpish green salad.

Serves 12

- 2¼ pounds (1 kg) small white haricot beans
- 2 large bouquets garnis
- 2 large onions–1 stuck with a few cloves
- 1 large carrot
- 8-ounce (225-g) piece cured ham or smoked belly of pork
- 18 cloves of garlic, 12 unpeeled, the rest peeled
- 12 black peppercorns
- 8 ounces (225 g) thickly cut smoked bacon

- 1-pound (450-g) can goose or duck *confit*
- 1 pound (450 g) canned tomatoes
- 2½ cups (600 ml) cups good strong stock
- a few sprigs of thyme

- 1 tablespoon (15 ml) strong Dijon mustard (optional)
- few drops of chili or Worcestershire sauce (definitely optional)
- small glass of brandy (optional)
- 12 spicy country sausages (Toulouse or Cumberland)
- a small bunch of parsley
- 1½ cups (90 g) white breadcrumbs made from day-old bread

SOAK THE HARICOT BEANS IN PLENTY OF cold water for at least 6 hours. Drain, rinse, and bring to a boil in plenty of fresh cold water, with 1 bouquet garni, the clove-studded onion, carrot, piece of ham or smoked belly of pork, 12 unpeeled garlic cloves, and the peppercorns.

Reduce the heat and simmer gently, half-covered, for about 1½ hours until the beans are cooked but still a little firm.

Meanwhile, chop the remaining onion and garlic and the smoked bacon. In a large, heavy-bottomed Dutch oven, brown the onion in a little of the goose or duck fat from the *confit*. Skin the meat and cut into small pieces. Stir the pieces into the browned onion with the chopped bacon and garlic; discard the skin. Add the bones to the bean mixture. Cook for a few minutes, stirring, then pour in the tomatoes with their juice and the stock. Add the second bouquet garni, the thyme, and any optional extras. Stir, cover, and cook gently for 20 to 30 minutes. Very slowly broil the sausages until crisp all over and cooked through, then cut into fork-size chunks.

Now, to assemble the *cassoulet*. Drain the beans and discard the onion, bones, bouquets garnis, and peppercorns. Chop up the carrot, and ham or pork (discarding the fat). If you are going to serve the *cassoulet* in the Dutch oven, transfer the meat stew to a bowl. Ladle a good layer of beans into the Dutch oven. Add half the carrot and ham or pork, then half the meat stew. Repeat the process, stretching the meat stew with extra hot water if it looks too thick and dry. Top with the remaining beans and the sausages. The *cassoulet* can be put aside at this stage, for up to 24 hours in a cool place.

To finish, snip the parsley into a bowl. Sprinkle the *cassoulet* with the breadcrumbs and parsley, then dot with some of the remaining duck/goose *confit*. About 45 to 60 minutes before serving, heat the oven to 400°F. Cover the *cassoulet* and heat for 20 minutes, then remove the lid and allow to brown for 20 minutes more. Serve very hot.

GIGOT
Leg of Lamb

ONE WORD OF CAUTION: You may be disappointed, but I am not going to offer a proper recipe for the greatest of all French festive meat dishes. *Gigot* has to be boldly cooked; there can be few adjustments and no camouflage. And the list of variables to be taken into consideration is more daunting than usual. First there is the lamb itself, and the way it is butchered and prepared. Then comes the roasting pan or dish, and the oven with its own little quirks and tricks. Last but not least, we have the cook, the carver, and the guests, with their different hands and palates. And when *gigot* is at stake, in my experience, people always have strong views and great expectations. Quite rightly so. After all, *gigot* is the food of high days and holidays.

I HAVE EATEN OTHER PEOPLE'S PERFECT *gigot* and made a quiet note of it. I have on occasion achieved my idea of *gigot* bliss, only to be met by barely polite noises around my table. So rather than a recipe, let me tell you what works for me.

In an ideal world, I will use young Welsh or English lamb, butchered and trimmed French-style, studded with lots of garlic, well seasoned, and rubbed with rosemary and thyme. I would have discussed the meat with my butcher, then decided whether or not to sit the *gigot* on a few good knobs of butter.

Before I put my *gigot* in the hot oven, I would dribble a little olive oil over it, then cook it very fast, basting a few times with the juices and a trickle of white wine.

Meanwhile, I would plead with the rest of the family, who like their lamb ultra-pink, for the *gigot* to be granted an extra few minutes in the oven, and, hopefully, for injury time afterward to relax. In the end I would serve it with *haricots verts* (see page 128), young flageolets (see page 129), and garlic sauce. And for these three items at least I can certainly provide recipes.

SAUCE À L'AIL
Garlic Sauce

DON'T BE PUT OFF by the 8 ounces (225 g) garlic I use in this recipe. It is not a printing error, and this easy-to-prepare sauce is more aromatic than pungent, because the garlic will be boiled three times. You'll also find that peeling the cooked cloves is a real cinch: Simply squeeze them between your thumb and forefinger and they'll just pop out.

8 ounces (225 g) cloves of
  garlic
1¼ cups (300 ml) light cream

Serves 6

sea salt
freshly ground black pepper

IN A MEDIUM-SIZE SAUCEPAN FILLED WITH plenty of cold water, bring the cloves of garlic to a boil.

As soon as the water starts bubbling, drain the cloves. Then return them to the pan, cover with fresh cold water, and bring to a boil again. Drain, then repeat the process one more time.

Now squeeze the softened cloves (see above). Combine the cream and the peeled cloves in the saucepan and heat through gently until piping hot but not boiling, stirring occasionally. Purée the mixture, season with a little salt and more generously with freshly ground black pepper and serve with *gigot*. This sauce can be reheated if necessary.

AGNEAU EN PAPILLOTE
Marinated Lamb in Foil

A RECIPE I HAVE USED and liked for years, from I-am-not-quite sure where in Provence. I serve this dish with rice, pasta, and tomatoes wilted in a low oven for 1 hour with Mediterranean herbs and a pinch of sugar, or with tiny young flageolets (see page 129) when they are around.

2 pounds (900 g) boned shoulder of lamb	**Serves 4**	a few fennel seeds 1 bay leaf
1 large ripe tomato	a couple of sprigs each of	a few mint leaves
1 large unwaxed lemon	thyme, marjoram, oregano,	freshly ground black pepper
5 tablespoons (75 ml) virgin olive oil	and rosemary	sea salt

TRIM THE FAT OFF THE MEAT, THEN CUT the shoulder into 12 pieces, not too small but no larger than 1½ inches (4 cm). Blanch the tomato in boiling water, then skin, and remove the seeds and pulp and chop the flesh. Grate and squeeze the lemon.

In a soup plate or shallow bowl, combine the olive oil with the chopped tomato and the grated zest and juice of the lemon. Snip in the herbs. Add a few fennel seeds, then snip in the bay leaf and the mint leaves. Season with freshly ground black pepper. Carefully roll the pieces of lamb in this marinade until they are coated all over. Cover

and leave to marinate for 2 hours at room temperature, or longer in the refrigerator.

Heat the oven to 425°F with a baking sheet in it. Cut 4 squares of foil, each large enough to comfortably wrap around 3 pieces of lamb. Put 3 pieces of marinated lamb in the center of each square of foil. Spoon any remaining marinade over the lamb. Season with a little salt and extra pepper. Close the packages, but not too tightly. Put them on the hot baking sheet.

Cook for 20 to 25 minutes and leave the meat to settle for 10 minutes before you open the foil packages.

Navarin D'Agneau
Lamb Stew with Turnips

A TRUSTED LAMB STEW. Feel free to vary the vegetables. The turnips are a traditional ingredient, but I sometimes replace them with potatoes, then add leeks and tomatoes halfway through the cooking.

Serves 6

2¼ pounds (1 kg) boned lamb
   shoulder or chump
freshly ground black pepper
1 large white Spanish onion
8 ounces (225 g) carrots
1 pound (450 g) turnips
2 or 3 cloves of garlic
1 tablespoon (15 ml) oil
2 teaspoons (10 g) flour

1¼ cups (300 ml) light beef
   stock or water
6 tablespoons (90 ml) dry white
   wine
several sprigs of parsley and
   rosemary
sea salt
1 tablespoon (15 g) butter, or
   1 tablespoon cream, to finish,
   if liked

TRIM A GOOD DEAL OF THE VISIBLE FAT from the meat. Cut it into 2-inch (5-cm) pieces. Sprinkle the pieces with finely ground black pepper and set aside while you prepare the vegetables. Coarsely chop the onion; trim and peel the carrots and the turnips. Cut into chunks; crush the garlic.

Heat the oil in a Dutch oven or large sauté pan. Over a moderately high heat, sauté the meat until lightly colored, then add the vegetables and sauté for a few minutes, stirring frequently. Sprinkle the flour over the dish and stir to mix it in. Then pour in the stock and the white wine.

Bring the liquid to a simmer, then snip in the herbs and season with salt and freshly ground black pepper. Cover, reduce the heat, and cook for about 1½ hours. Skim off the surface fat and scum occasionally.

Once the stew is cooked, remove the meat and vegetables from the pot with a draining spoon; keep them warm. Skim off any fat, then strain the liquid and return it to the pot, turn up the heat, and reduce a little. Check the seasoning. Swirl in a knob of butter or a spoonful of cream, if you wish, then return the meat and vegetables to the pot, stir them in well and serve immediately.

TAGINE DE MOUTON YONNÉE
Pot-Roasted Lamb with Onions and Raisins

THE PAST IS ANOTHER COUNTRY and like everyone else I have always been intrigued by my parents' past, the remote land of before my time. My father and his brothers spent a few happy years as children in North Africa. He returned during the war after escaping from a German POW camp. There he met up with his brother, Jean, and sister-in-law, Yonnée. They were all actively working for the Free French. These were dangerous but exciting days, and I have never tired of hearing about them. Many of the North African stories were told around a *couscous* or *tagine*, and over a glass of Boulaouane grayish rosé wine. This recipe of my aunt's is as simple as it is delectable and should be served with rice.

Serves 6

⅓ cup (45 g) raisins
1 cup (250 ml) of cold, weak
    tea
2¾ to 3 pounds (1.2 to 1.4 kg)
    shoulder of mature lamb
3 tablespoons (45 ml) olive oil
2½ large unwaxed lemons
1 good pinch of powdered
    saffron
1 tablespoon (15 g) powdered
    cumin
3 cloves of garlic
sea salt
freshly ground black pepper
2 pounds (900 g) large white
    Spanish onions

SOAK THE RAISINS IN WEAK TEA OVERNIGHT or for several hours. Trim most of the visible fat from the lamb, then cut it into 2-inch (5-cm) pieces.

Grease a Dutch oven with a little olive oil. Grate and squeeze 1 lemon. Put the meat pieces in the casserole, then sprinkle in the lemon juice and zest, the saffron, and the cumin. Add the garlic. Chop up another lemon and add it. Season lightly with salt and freshly ground black pepper. Cover, and very slowly cook over an extremely low heat for 3 hours.

After about 2½ hours, thinly slice the onions. Heat the rest of the olive oil in a sauté pan and very gently sweat and cook the onions. Stir them frequently and do not let them turn brown. Drain the raisins. When the onions are nearly done, stir in the drained raisins.

Add the onions and raisins to the lamb, stir and cook together for a few minutes. Squeeze the remaining half lemon and sprinkle the juice over the dish. Stir and check the seasoning. This dish should be served piping hot.

ROGNONS AU VIN ROUGE
Kidneys in Red Wine

A QUICK AND tasty dish that is good with plain rice.

1 pound (450 g) lamb's kidneys	Serves 4	freshly ground black pepper
3 shallots		grated nutmeg
1 clove of garlic		2 teaspoons (10 g) flour
1 tablespoon (15 ml) oil		2 teaspoons (10 ml) mild Dijon
2 tablespoons (30 g) butter		mustard
½ cup (120 ml) red wine		2 tablespoons (30 ml) heavy
1 bay leaf		cream
sea salt		several sprigs of fresh parsley

MAKE THE SAUCE. FINELY CHOP THE shallots and garlic. Heat half the oil and a good knob of butter in a heavy-bottomed saucepan. Sweat the shallots and garlic over a low heat until soft, without allowing them to color. Pour in the red wine and 3 tablespoons of cold water. Add the bay leaf and simmer gently for 5 minutes, stirring occasionally.

Finally, season with a little salt, freshly ground black pepper, and a small pinch of grated nutmeg.

While the sauce is cooking, prepare the kidneys. Rinse them well under cold running water, then pat dry with paper towels and trim off any skin and core. Cut each kidney in half lengthwise. Melt the rest of the butter in a skillet. Dust the kidneys with flour, then sauté them over a moderately high heat for 3 to 4 minutes on each side, until they stiffen a little and change color.

Remove the kidneys from the pan with a draining spoon and keep warm.

Pour the sauce into the skillet, and stir it in thoroughly, scraping up the pan sediments. Add the mustard and the cream and stir in well, then return the kidneys and their juices to the pan. Stir until heated through.

Snip the parsley and sprinkle over the kidneys. To enjoy this dish at its peak, serve immediately.

BŒUF BOURGUIGNON
Beef Cooked in Red Burgundy

SINCE THIS DISH is infinitely better reheated, I always make it the day before. The last-minute addition of brandy, wine, and butter brings the *bourguignon* alive and literally makes the sauce shine.

	Serves 4	
2 pounds (900 g) chuck or blade steak		1 bottle Burgundy or similar style wine
2 thickly cut slices smoked bacon		sea salt
1 large white Spanish onion	1 tablespoon (15 g) flour	freshly ground black pepper
1 clove of garlic	a few sprigs of thyme	1 tablespoon (15 ml) brandy
1 tablespoon (15 ml) oil	1 bay leaf	2 tablespoons (30 g) butter
		several sprigs of fresh parsley

BULL'S HEAD.

PREFERABLY START COOKING THE DISH ON the day before you intend to eat it. Trim any surplus fat off the beef. Cut the meat into chunks, not bigger than 2 inches (5 cm) square. Chop the bacon and onion, and crush the garlic. Heat the oil in a Dutch oven or large sauté pan. Sauté the bacon until it turns brown. Turn up the heat a bit, add the beef and brown quickly on all sides.

Remove the meat from the pan with a draining spoon. Add the onion and sauté until it colors. Return the meat to the pan, add the garlic, and sprinkle with the flour. Stir for a few minutes, then add the thyme, bay leaf, and three-quarters of the bottle of wine. Season with salt, more generously with freshly ground black pepper, and bring to a simmer, stirring occasionally.

Now reduce the heat to very low, cover tightly, and cook extremely slowly for at least 2½ hours, giving the mixture an occasional stir. Turn off the heat and leave overnight to mature.

The next day, very gently reheat the dish for about 40 minutes. Carefully take out the meat with tongs or a draining spoon and put it on a plate, or if you prefer, pile it on a serving dish. Then turn up the heat a little, stir in the brandy and continue to cook for a few minutes.

Meanwhile, snip the parsley. Pour the rest of the wine into the pan, swirl in the butter, and stir, then either return the meat to the pan or pour the sauce over the meat in the serving dish. Sprinkle with the parsley and serve immediately.

BŒUF EN DAUBE
Slow-Cooked Beef Casserole

ONE OF MY FAVORITE French country casseroles, and very different in texture and flavor. Unlike *bœuf bourguignon*, this dish is best served with rice or pasta, rather than potatoes.

2¼ pounds (1 kg) braising steak	**Serves 5 or 6**	2 cloves of garlic
1 large white Spanish onion		2 large ripe tomatoes
1 shallot	3 tablespoons (45 ml) olive oil	12 black olives
2 bay leaves	about 2¼ cups (550 ml) light	7 ounces (200 g) mushrooms
several sprigs each of thyme	red or white wine	sea salt
and parsley	4 thickly cut slices of smoked	freshly ground black pepper
a few black peppercorns	bacon	

TRIM ANY VISIBLE FAT OFF THE MEAT, then cut into 2-inch (5-cm) chunks. Chop the onion and shallot. In a large bowl, combine the meat, onion, shallot, bay leaves, thyme, parsley, and peppercorns with half the oil and just enough red wine to cover; leave to marinate overnight.

The next day, heat the oven to 325°F. Chop the bacon. In a Dutch oven, heat the rest of the oil. Add the bacon and sauté until it begins to brown. Take the meat out of the marinade, reserving the marinade. Drain the meat well and pat dry with a clean cloth or paper towels. Add the meat to the dish and brown on all sides for a few minutes over a moderately high heat.

Coarsely chop the garlic and tomatoes. Pit and chop the olives, and wipe and slice the mushrooms. Add all these to the dish together with the onion and shallot from the marinade; stir well.

Cover the dish tightly and cook in the oven for 20 minutes.

Take the dish out of the oven and pour in the reserved marinade. Season to taste with salt and freshly ground black pepper. Stir thoroughly, cover the dish tightly again, and return to the oven.

Turn the oven down to 250°F. Cook for a good 3 hours, occasionally checking to see that there is still enough wine to come halfway up the pieces of meat. Add a little extra wine if necessary. Serve hot. Leftovers are delicious cold.

Pot au Feu
Boiled Beef with Vegetables

THE GRAND OLD one-pot meal of France—and a good way to make a proper light beef stock. In my experience, there is never a great deal of leftover beef, but what there might be is excellent served cold with a garlicky mayonnaise.

There never seems to be enough marrow either. When I was a child, the precious substance was always ceremoniously given on a piece of toast to my grandmother, while we all wondered what on earth the fuss was about.

Serves 8

2¼ pounds (1 kg) lean braising beef
2¼ pounds (1 kg) shin of beef, meat and bone
1 large marrow bone
3 cloves of garlic
2 bay leaves
several sprigs of thyme
6 carrots
4 turnips

4 medium-size potatoes
8 button onions
4 large leeks
4 stalks of celery
sea salt

several sprigs each of chervil and parsley
freshly ground black pepper

TO SERVE
strong Dijon mustard
coarse-grain mustard
coarse kosher salt
gherkins
creamed horseradish

INTO YOUR LARGEST, HEAVY-BOTTOMED saucepan or stockpot, put the meat bones. Trim off most of the visible fat, then cut the meat into large pieces—no smaller than about 3 inches (7.5 cm) square—and tie them together. Put the meat on top of the bones. Cover with plenty of cold water, add the garlic, bay leaves, and thyme and very slowly bring to a boil over an extremely low heat. Skim off any grayish scum as soon as it comes up to the surface.

While the meat is coming to a boil, carefully prepare the vegetables. Peel the carrots and cut them into segments. Peel the turnips and cut in half, or quarter them if they are large. Peel the potatoes and cut in half. Peel the onions neatly. Trim the leeks, cut in half lengthwise and rinse them well. Trim and rinse the stalks of celery. Tie together the leeks and celery into 3 bundles.

Add the carrots, turnips, and potatoes to the pan. Bring back to a very gentle boil and skim off any scum. Season lightly with salt. Now add the onions and the leek and celery bundles. Bring back to a low boil, skim again, and partly cover. Cook very slowly for at least another 2½ hours, skimming until any foam that comes up looks light and white. Add the parsley and chervil after about 1 hour of cooking.

Remove from the heat and leave to settle for a few minutes. Remove any surface fat with a spoon. Lift out the meat and vegetables with a draining spoon. Discard the strings, then heap meat and vegetables attractively on a serving dish. Spoon out the marrow and reserve for your most honored or senior guest; discard the bones.

Strain the stock through a strainer lined with cheesecloth or a clean fine cloth into a saucepan. Bring to a simmer, add a little freshly ground black pepper and salt, if necessary, and moisten the meat and vegetables with a little sauce. Pour some more stock into a bowl to serve with the dish. Have on the table at the same time different kinds of mustards, coarse salt, and creamed horseradish.

Bœuf Mode
Braised Beef

Bœuf mode can be served hot or cold, which I much prefer. It makes a splendid party dish.

Serves 8

1 calf's foot, split in half
4 thickly cut slices of smoked back bacon
4 pounds (1.8 kg) rolled topside of beef, larded and barded

1¼ cups (300 ml) dry white wine, plus extra, if needed
2 cloves of garlic
several sprigs of parsley and thyme

2 or 3 bay leaves
sea salt
freshly ground black pepper
about 24 pearl onions
1 pound (450 g) baby carrots

Rinse and scrub the calf's foot, then blanch it for a few minutes in boiling water. Drain the foot and, if you wish and possess a cleaver or heavy knife, cut into pieces. Chop the bacon.

Place a large Dutch oven over a moderate heat. Add the chopped bacon to the pot and sauté until the juices begin to run. Add the beef and brown lightly and evenly on all sides. Now add the calf's foot and moisten with the white wine and about the same quantity of water. Chop or crush the garlic and add to the dish with the sprigs of herbs and the bay leaves. Season lightly with salt and freshly ground black pepper. Cover tightly and cook over a very low heat for a good 2 hours.

After about 2 hours, peel and trim the onions. Scrape the baby carrots and cut into segments. Add the onions and carrots to the pan with a little extra wine and water if the level of the liquid looks too low. Cover and cook for 1½ hours more over a low heat.

If you want to eat this dish hot, leave the pot off the heat for at least 10 minutes, and skim the fat off the surface before serving. Chill any remains: The jellied leftovers will be excellent served cold the following day.

To serve the whole dish cold, allow the beef to cool in the pot until barely warm. Remove it from the pot and leave to get cold on a large plate, then cover it with foil and chill for a couple of hours. Strain the liquid, reserving the vegetables and the pieces of calf's foot. Leave the liquid to get cold and then chill. Also refrigerate the vegetables and calf's foot.

Remove the strings and the outer fat from the chilled beef and cut it into thin slices. Arrange the slices on a large serving dish, so that they overlap attractively. Surround with the reserved vegetables and pieces of calf's foot. Spoon the jellied or syrupy sauce over the dish, and sprinkle very lightly with freshly ground black pepper. Cover the dish with plastic wrap or foil and chill until ready to serve.

STEAKS AU POIVRE ET AUX ANCHOIS
Steaks with Pepper and Anchovy

ONE OF MY FAVORITE "quickie" sauces. My husband is more a steak-eater than I, and he believes in warming the steaks in a little butter before patting in the crushed peppercorns. It does seem to deepen the peppery flavor, but since Colin got the idea from a James Beard book I am only mentioning this as an aside and for the sake of *entente cordiale* and *matrimoniale*.

Serves 4

4 steaks, from the tenderloin or
   sirloin, about 1½ inches
   (4 cm) thick
2 level tablespoons (30 g) black
   peppercorns
1 tablespoon (15 ml) oil
4 tablespoons (60 g) butter
2 tablespoons (30 ml) dry white
   wine
3 tablespoons (45 ml) *crème
   fraîche* or heavy cream
2 teaspoons (10 ml) anchovy
   paste
1 tablespoon (15 ml) brandy

AT LEAST 1 HOUR BEFORE YOU WANT TO start cooking the steaks, crush the peppercorns with the help of a mortar and pestle. Sprinkle the crushed peppercorns over the steaks, then press them in firmly with your hands. Cover with plastic wrap and set aside at room temperature.

Meanwhile, in a large, heavy-bottomed skillet, heat the oil and a good knob of butter over a high heat. Cut the rest of the butter into small pieces. Then add the steaks and cook them for 2 to 4 minutes on each side, depending on your taste and the thickness, and cut, of the meat.

Put the steaks on a hot serving dish. Now swirl the wine into the pan, stir it for a minute, scraping the bottom of the pan, then add the cream and anchovy paste. Stir the sauce until it is heated through, and swirl in the brandy.

Away from the heat, swirl in the pieces of chopped-up butter. Then pour the sauce over the steaks on their serving dish and serve at once.

HACHIS PARMENTIER
French Cottage Pie

THERE IS ABSOLUTELY no reason to turn up one's nose (however refined) at leftover beef when it is done this way. Having said that, I must admit that bland *hachis parmentier*, thriftily made from plain ground cooked beef and thin potato purée, is a pretty mean-spirited concoction. The one we did at home wasn't particularly economical, but it did taste good. And very often I much preferred it to the roast it originated from.

2 thickly cut slices of smoked
    bacon
1 smallish onion
2 shallots
1 clove of garlic
1 tablespoon (15 ml) olive oil
4 tablespoons (60 g) butter
about 12 ounces (350 g)
    cooked beef

Serves 4 or 5

4 tablespoons (60 ml) red wine
sea salt
freshly ground black pepper
a pinch of cayenne pepper or
    other ground chili

a dash of Worcestershire sauce
a dash of tomato ketchup
about 2½ cups (350 g) not too
    heavy *purée de pommes de
    terre* (see page 123)
1½ ounces (45 g) Gruyère
    cheese
¾ cup (45 g) breadcrumbs
    made from day-old bread

BRIEFLY WHIZZ TOGETHER THE BACON, onion, shallots, and garlic in a food processor. Heat the oil with a knob of butter in a skillet. Brown the bacon, onion, and garlic mixture over a fairly high heat. Meanwhile, quickly process the cooked beef. Add the beef to the pan, stir it in well, and sauté for a couple of minutes, still over a fairly high heat.

Heat the oven to 450°F. Pour the wine into the skillet and season to taste with salt and freshly ground black pepper. Add a little cayenne or chili, and a dash of Worcestershire sauce and the ketchup. Reduce the heat a little and simmer for 10 minutes, stirring occasionally.

Butter a gratin dish. Spread a thin layer of creamed potato over the bottom of the dish. Cover with an even layer of beef hash. Cover with the rest of the potato. Grate the Gruyère over the dish and sprinkle with the breadcrumbs. Dot with the rest of the butter. Bake for 15 minutes until the topping is golden brown. Serve immediately.

LÉGUMES
Vegetables

WHENEVER THEY COME back from a holiday in France, my American and English vegetarian friends are always quick to point out that they find eating in the average French restaurant rather a depressing experience.

They explain vividly that there are very few vegetables on menus–never mind vegetarian dishes. I make patriotic excuses, of course, but to some extent I sympathize with them. A couple of year ago, traveling around the Toulouse–Albi region and eating in restaurants that the locals treated as their canteens, I soon wondered where all the vegetables were. This was September and the markets were bursting with vivid colors and mellow produce. But here we were, everywhere we went, being offered five-course menus that were incredibly high on value and animal protein. Withdrawal symptoms soon set in and I got to munching tomatoes in the car. After a few days, when we got to Cahors, I was overwhelmed with joy to discover that it had one vegetarian restaurant. It was tucked away near the cathedral, a throwback to the Seventies in its treatment of nut rissoles and general décor. But, how wonderful, at last, to be able to savor a meal built on the wealth of vegetables I had admired at the markets.

To eat vegetables in France, you have to go to someone's home. Depending on whether it is lunch or dinner, you'll begin the meal with crudités or soup, probably have potatoes or maybe plain rice or pasta with the main course, then almost certainly a green salad. A separate vegetable course is a strong possibility in the evening, particularly if the meal does not include meat. In fact, provided they eat eggs as well, I think my vegetarian friends would very much enjoy supper in a French home.

RATATOUILLE
Ragout of Provençal Vegetables

RATATOUILLE TASTES BEST in late summer when vegetables are at their peak of ripeness. There is a painstaking way of making *ratatouille*, which involves sautéing the vegetables separately before the final assembly. It produces an excellent *ratatouille*, but it takes infinitely longer than the recipe below. And somehow I don't think the end result justifies the effort. I prefer this slightly coarser version. If nothing else, it is closer in spirit to the name of the dish: *touiller* is a slangy way of saying stir or mix. As for *rata*, any French conscript will tell you that it just means plain old army grub.

Ratatouille is particularly good served with a plain omelet.

Serves 4 to 6

2 medium-size eggplants
    (aubergines)
3 cloves of garlic
6 tablespoons (90 ml) olive oil
2 sweet red bell peppers
1 large white onion
6 small zucchini
2 large ripe tomatoes
a few sprigs of thyme, sweet
    savory, marjoram, and
    oregano
sea salt
freshly ground black pepper
several sprigs of parsley

PEEL THE EGGPLANTS AND CUT THEM crosswise into thin slices. Cut one of the cloves of garlic and use it to rub a wide heavy-bottomed saucepan or sauté pan. Crush the rest of the garlic.

Heat 2 tablespoons of olive oil in the pan. Sauté the sliced eggplants for a few minutes.

Meanwhile, core and thinly slice the peppers. Add the peppers to the pan and sauté gently for a few minutes, until softened; take care not to overcook them.

Slice the onion very thinly. Add another tablespoon of olive oil to the pan, then stir in the onion rings. Sauté for a few minutes, stirring occasionally.

Meanwhile, cut the zucchini, then blanch, peel, seed, and chop the tomatoes. Stir the zucchini into the pan. Sauté for a couple of minutes, then add the chopped tomatoes and the crushed garlic. Snip in the thyme, sweet savory, marjoram, and oregano; season lightly with salt and freshly ground black pepper. Stir in another 2 tablespoons of olive oil and cover the pan. Reduce the heat a little and cook very gently for 30 to 40 minutes, stirring occasionally.

Snip in the parsley and add 1 more table-spoon of olive oil. Continue cooking on a low heat for 5 to 10 minutes. Check the seasoning. Serve hot, warm, or cold, as you prefer.

GRATIN DAUPHINOIS
Potato Gratin

DAUPHINOIS, THE GREATEST GRATIN of them all, is a traditional accompaniment to roasts. In my opinion, at its creamy luxurious best, it deserves to be a course in its own right.

Gratin dauphinois is another of those dishes that no two people will ever make exactly the same. Mado, my grandmother's cook, first taught me a *gratin* made with thickly cut potatoes, milk, no eggs, and good knobs of butter. My mother preferred thick slices of potato, 2 eggs, and a mixture of milk and *crème fraîche*. I now find that if I am using cream, the *gratin* works best with thin slices, and if milk, thick slices . . . Ah well. One egg yolk does help though, and the good thing is, you can't really go wrong anyway.

Serves 6 to 8

2 pounds (900 g) large waxy
    potatoes
2 or 3 cloves of garlic
butter
2¼ cups (550 ml) full-fat milk,
    or 2 cups (450 ml) light
    cream, or a mixture of the
    two
1 egg yolk
a pinch of grated nutmeg
sea salt
freshly ground black pepper

HEAT THE OVEN TO 325°F. PEEL THE potatoes and slice them evenly–I do this with the slicing disk of the food processor. Leave to drain in a colander for 5 to 10 minutes, patting dry with paper towels. Cut the cloves of garlic. Rub a gratin dish thoroughly with the cut sides of the cloves, then crush the garlic. Generously grease the dish with butter.

Gently warm the milk, cream, or mixture of both in a saucepan. Whisk in the egg yolk and stir in a pinch of nutmeg. Season with a little salt and freshly ground black pepper.

Spread a layer of potatoes in the prepared dish. Scatter some of the crushed garlic over them and season lightly. Spoon or trickle in a little of the milk or cream mixture. Repeat until all the potatoes are used up, ending with a good layer of milk or cream. Dot the surface with several little knobs of butter.

Cook in the oven for 1 hour, then turn up the heat to 400°F, and cook for 20 to 30 minutes more, until the *gratin* is golden brown and the potatoes tender: This you can test with a skewer.

If the potatoes aren't quite done, reduce the heat to the original setting and cook for another 15 minutes.

Purée de Pommes de Terre Marthe
Creamed Potatoes

Marthe was my family's maid in Paris and was quite a character. She had left school at 12, but she wrote well-turned sentences in a fine hand and could be relied on to advise us on grammar. She wore dentures that fascinated us, and she had a strange habit of piecing together torn-up letters from wastepaper baskets. One day she confronted my father with one such discarded message. She was livid. How *could* Monsieur . . . Monsieur had so hated the Camembert at supper the previous evening that he had written a sarcastic note to Marthe to that effect–he always left for work before she arrived. Naturally he had soon thought better of it and torn up the note. We girls sided with her. How could anyone be so cruel, even if he changed his mind later. Marthe made the best creamed potatoes I have ever tasted, deceptively light and totally irresistible. This is more or less her recipe–rather less than more, because I use a little less egg and butter.

2½ pounds (1.1 kg) floury potatoes sea salt 6½ tablespoons (100 ml) milk 1 tablespoon (15 ml) cream	**Serves 6 to 8**	4 tablespoons (60 g) butter, plus extra to finish, if liked 1 egg yolk freshly ground black pepper

Bring a large saucepan of lightly salted water to a boil. Peel the potatoes and cut them in half, or quarters if they are very large. Add the potatoes to the boiling water and bring it back to a boil. Reduce the heat a little and simmer gently until the potatoes are cooked, but not mushy. Do not let the water bubble too fast, or the potatoes will cook unevenly and disintegrate.

Meanwhile, heat the milk in a small saucepan until very hot, but not quite boiling; drain the potatoes well. Pass them through a *mouli* or mash lightly with a potato masher. Return the potatoes to the pan, with the butter, and stir gently over a low heat to remove the excess moisture.

Whisk in half the hot milk, then the cream, working vigorously. Beat the egg into the last few spoonfuls of milk, and whisk this into the potatoes; season to taste. If you like, swirl in a good knob of butter. Serve at once.

The purée should not really be reheated (except when making *hachis parmentier*, page 119). But it will keep warm for up to 15 minutes in a bowl, covered with a heated plate, set over a pan of very hot water.

POMMES DE TERRE SAUTÉES
TATA BOUCHER
Sautéed Potatoes

I HAVE ALREADY mentioned Madame Boucher, she of the magnificent omelets. Her sautéed potatoes were equally satisfying. Perhaps this is why in our gratefulness we dubbed her Tata: Although not our aunt or great-aunt, she was an honorary and honored member of the family.

2¼ pounds (1 kg) waxy
  potatoes
5 tablespoons (75 ml) oil
3 tablespoons (45 g) butter

Serves 6

sea salt
freshly ground black pepper
several sprigs of parsley

PEEL THE POTATOES AND CUT THEM INTO small dice, about ¾ inch (2 cm) and certainly no larger than 1 inch. Rinse the diced potatoes in hot water, drain well, and dry them thoroughly with a clean cloth or paper towels–this seems to prevent the potatoes from sticking together during cooking.

In a very large, heavy-bottomed skillet, heat the oil and butter. Add the potatoes–the pan should be large enough to take them very comfortably more or less in a single layer; otherwise use 2 pans.

Season liberally with salt and pepper. Over a low heat sauté the potatoes until crisp and golden; this may take up to 1 hour. Turn the heat down if the potatoes are browning too much. Stir frequently with a wooden spatula and give the pan an occasional good shake. Snip the parsley into a bowl and add the potatoes. They won't need draining but if they look even remotely greasy, drain them on paper towels. Check the seasoning, and sprinkle the potatoes with extra snipped parsley. Serve hot.

POIREAUX À LA CRÈME
Leeks with Cream

THIS IS A GOOD VEGETABLE DISH to bear in mind if you know you are going to be pushed for time at the last minute. The softened leeks will happily keep for several hours. Reheat and finish off just before serving. Delicious with fish, particularly as a bed for seabass.

2¼ pounds (1 kg) leeks
4 tablespoons (60 g) butter
sea salt

Serves 6

freshly ground black pepper
2 to 3 tablespoons (30 to 45 ml)
  crème fraîche or sour cream

TRIM THE LEEKS. SLIT THEM LENGTHWISE, and wash thoroughly in cold water. Drain well, dry with paper towels, and chop. Melt the butter in a sauté pan, then stir in the leeks.

Cover and cook over a low heat until soft (20 minutes). Shake the pan often. Season with salt and freshly ground black pepper. Stir in the *crème fraîche* or sour cream. Serve hot.

Petits Pois à la Laitue et aux Petits Oignons

Baby Peas with Lettuce and Onions

Fresh from the garden, *petits pois* have always been one of the joys of the summer table. I sometimes add one or two chopped slices of unsmoked bacon to the other ingredients at the beginning of the recipe.

4½ pounds (2 kg) unshelled, or
   3½ cups (500 g) shelled baby
   peas
4 tablespoons (60 g) butter
2 tender lettuces
1 mild onion, or 2 small onions

Serves 4

⅔ cup (150 ml) light chicken
   stock or water
1 teaspoon (5 g) sugar
sea salt
freshly ground black pepper

Shell the peas. Melt the butter in a heavy-bottomed saucepan. Wash and coarsely shred the lettuces. Peel and very thinly slice the onion or onions. Add the peas, lettuces, and onion to the pan. Stir to coat in butter, then cover. Cook very gently over a low heat for 5 to 10 minutes, shaking the pan occasionally.

Add the stock or cold water and sprinkle in the sugar. Season with a little salt and freshly ground black pepper.

Cover and cook over a low heat for 10 to 15 minutes until the peas are tender. Taste and adjust the seasoning. Drain well and serve immediately.

Carottes au Cumin

Carrots Cooked with Cumin

A good way to cook mature carrots.

2¾ pounds (1.2 kg) carrots
2 to 3 tablespoons (30 to 45 ml)
   olive oil
1 teaspoon (5 g) ground cumin
sea salt

Serves 6

freshly ground black pepper
1 or 2 cloves of garlic
3 tablespoons (45 ml) white
   wine

Peel and slice the carrots. Heat the oil in a sauté pan. Add the carrots and cumin, season lightly with salt and freshly ground black pepper, and cook over a low heat for about 15 minutes, stirring occasionally.

Crush the garlic and add to the pan. Stir well, then moisten with the white wine and a glass of water. Cover and cook very gently for 45 minutes, shaking the pan from time to time. Drain and serve hot.

Emincé de Carottes et de Courgettes

Sautéed Carrot and Zucchini Ribbons

Watching cooks going about their kitchen is the best way to learn. When I saw my sister Anne-Sophie Naudin prepare this pretty combination of faintly sweet, tender vegetables livened up by shallots and a splash of vermouth, I knew this was a dish I would do again and again–perfect for when you want something a bit special to serve with fish or white meat.

Serves 6

1 pound (450 g) carrots
1 pound (450 g) zucchini
1½ tablespoons (22 ml) olive oil
1 ounce (30 g) butter
2 shallots

3 tablespoons (45 ml) Noilly-Prat, or other dry vermouth or dry sherry
1 tablespoon (15 ml) *crème fraîche*

2 tablespoons (30 ml) finely chopped parsley
sea salt and freshly ground black pepper

Grate the carrots and zucchini, using a food mill or food processor. In a large skillet, over a low heat, mix the oil with half the butter. Add the vegetables, season, and cook over a low heat for 10 minutes, stirring from time to time.

Peel and finely chop the shallots. Add to the pan, stir in the rest of the butter, and continue cooking and stirring occasionally for about 10 minutes until tender, keeping the heat low. Stir in the Noilly-Prat, cook for 2 minutes, then stir in the cream and parsley. Remove from the heat, adjust the seasoning, and serve hot.

GRATIN D'AUBERGINES
Eggplant Gratin

I often leave out the Gruyère to be able to enjoy the full Mediterranean flavors of the vegetables, but Gruyère featured in the original recipe and so stays in as an option. This is a good dish for vegetarians.

3 or 4 unblemished large, long
  eggplants
olive oil
1½ pounds (750 g) ripe
  tomatoes
2 or 3 cloves of garlic
several sprigs each of parsley,
  thyme, and chervil

Serves 6

a few sprigs of marjoram and
  oregano
1 to 2 teaspoons (5 to 10 g)
  sugar
sea salt
freshly ground black pepper
5 ounces (150 g) Gruyère
  cheese, if liked

WIPE THE EGGPLANTS. SLICE THEM THINLY lengthwise without peeling. Heat 1 tablespoon of olive oil in a large skillet. Sauté the eggplant slices over a moderate heat, a few at a time. Turn them over as soon as they become a little crisp and golden on the underside. Drain them well on a thick layer of paper towels, turning them over to mop up as much fat as possible.

Continue in the same way until all the eggplant slices have been sautéed, adding more oil as necessary. Turn down the heat a little after a while and resist any impulse to speed up the process–eggplants burn all too readily. At the same time blanch the tomatoes in boiling water, then peel them, cut in half, remove the seeds, and chop the flesh coarsely.

Crush the garlic. In the sauté pan, heat 1 tablespoon of olive oil. Tip in the tomatoes. Add the crushed garlic, snip in the herbs, and sprinkle in the sugar. Cook over a low heat until the mixture becomes a soft purée, stirring frequently. Season with a little salt and freshly ground black pepper. Heat the oven to 350°F. Grate the Gruyère, if using.

Put a layer of eggplant slices in the bottom of a gratin dish. Season lightly. Spread a thin layer of tomato purée over the eggplants. If you are using Gruyère, sprinkle a little on top of the tomatoes. Repeat until all the ingredients are used up. Sprinkle the top layer with a little olive oil. Cook in the oven for a good hour. Eat warm rather than hot, and preferably as a separate course.

Purée d'Oignons
Onion Purée

THIS SIDE DISH nicely accompanies plain roasts, broiled meat, and pan fries. It can be made well ahead and reheated at the last minute. I sometimes add a few cloves of garlic to the onions.

¼ cup (30 g) raisins
7 ounces (200 ml) hot weak tea
18 ounces (500 g) onions
2 tablespoons (30 ml)
   sunflower or peanut oil
2 tablespoons (30 g) sugar

Serves 6

6 tablespoons (90 ml) dry white
   wine
3 tablespoons (45 ml) white
   wine vinegar
sea salt
freshly ground black pepper

SOAK THE RAISINS IN THE HOT WEAK TEA. Meanwhile, coarsely chop the onions. Heat the oil in a saucepan. Over a low heat, gently sweat the onions in the oil, without letting them brown. Sprinkle in the sugar, stir, and cover. Reduce the heat to very low, cover, and cook for 15 minutes, occasionally shaking the pan.

Now add the wine. Stir, cover, and cook for another 15 minutes, still very gently. Stir in the vinegar and continue cooking for 10 minutes. Drain the raisins, and add them to the pan as well, season lightly, and cook for 15 minutes more. The onions will be meltingly soft and only lightly colored. Serve hot.

Haricots Verts Fourchettes
French Beans

ON SUMMER EVENINGS, at my grandparents' house, supper often consisted of vast platters of beans prepared this way. The exact amount of butter, garlic, and parsley varies with the cook. The quantities below are a moderate guideline.

18 ounces (500 g) young thin
   green beans
sea salt
1 small clove of garlic

Serves 4

several sprigs of parsley
3 tablespoons (45 g) butter
freshly ground black pepper

TOP AND TAIL THE BEANS AND REMOVE any strings. Bring a large saucepan of water to a boil and add a little salt. Throw in the beans, bring back to a boil, and keep it that way until the beans are cooked to your liking, but preferably still a little firm. While the beans are cooking, crush the garlic and snip the parsley into a bowl.

Have a big bowl of ice water ready. Quickly drain the beans and plunge into the ice water. Leave them in for a few seconds and drain again. Dry in a clean cloth if you like. Now melt the butter in a sauté pan. Add the beans to the butter with the garlic and parsley. Mix well, stir over a moderate heat and serve when heated through.

FLAGEOLETS AU NATUREL
Simple Flageolet Beans

A DISH I ONLY DO when I see really attractive, fresh-looking small flageolets, sometimes at my local health-food store in London, but more likely on a French market stall in the autumn. The rest of the time I am content enough with my cans (see page 130).

Ideal with *gigot* and good with duck, these flageolets (without the butter finish) also make the basis of a good salad. Dress with extra-virgin olive oil and lemon juice, add plenty of snipped scallions, chives, and parsley, then serve at room temperature.

18 ounces (500 g) young flageolet beans a few sprigs each of thyme and marjoram 3 sage leaves 1 bay leaf 1 clove of garlic	Serves 4 to 6	1½ quarts (1.5 liters) liquid made up from chicken stock and water sea salt freshly ground black pepper 3 tablespoons (45 g) butter several sprigs of fresh parsley

SOAK THE FLAGEOLETS FOR 1 TO 2 HOURS—the fresher they are, the less they will need to soak. Discard any damaged beans that come up to the surface; drain and rinse. Place the herbs and the garlic on a piece of cheesecloth. Form the cheesecloth into a little pouch, and secure it with fine string. Into a large, heavy-bottomed saucepan, pour the chicken stock and water. Add the flageolets and cheesecloth pouch.

Bring slowly to a boil and skim off any scum, then cover and simmer gently for 40 minutes. Season with salt and freshly ground black pepper. Cover again and continue to simmer gently until the flageolets are cooked and soft, skimming occasionally. This will probably take another 30 minutes at least; the exact timing will depend on the freshness and quality of the flageolets.

When the flageolets are cooked, drain them well. Swirl in the butter and snip in the parsley before serving.

HARICOTS EN BOÎTE AMÉLIORÉS
Improved Canned Haricot Beans

I WAS BROUGHT up not to have any qualms about using canned haricot and flageolet beans. Look for *flageolets extra fins* in particular. They are worth stocking up on and excellent with lamb, sausages, or bacon.

Serves 4

1-pound (450-g) can of
  flageolets or haricot beans
1 clove of garlic
1 large white Spanish onion or
  several pearl onions

1 large ripe tomato
1 tablespoon (15 ml) olive oil
1 tablespoon (15 g) butter
sea salt
freshly ground black pepper

DRAIN AND COPIOUSLY RINSE THE CANNED beans. Finely chop the garlic and the large onion, if using. If using pearl onions, blanch them for several minutes in boiling water; drain well. Blanch the tomato, then peel, seed, and chop it.

Heat the olive oil in a sauté pan. Add the garlic, prepared onion or pearl onions, and tomato. Sauté gently for a few minutes, until softened. Add the drained beans and 6 tablespoons of water. Heat through over a low heat, stirring a few times. Drain once the beans are hot. Tip into a serving dish, swirl in the butter and season to taste. Serve hot.

CHAMPIGNONS FARCIS
Stuffed Mushrooms

A GUTSY AND BUTTERY dish worth serving as a separate course.

Serves 4

4 very large or 8 medium-size
  undamaged, flat mushrooms
olive oil and butter for greasing

FOR THE STUFFING
8 tablespoons (120 g) butter
2 canned anchovy fillets or
  2 teaspoons (10 ml) anchovy
  paste
2 or 3 cloves of garlic

several sprigs each of parsley
  and chives
¾ cup (45 g) breadcrumbs
  made from day-old bread
sea salt
freshly ground black pepper

HEAT THE OVEN TO 375°F. WIPE THE mushrooms, and break or cut off the stems. Trim off the gritty bottom ends, then finely chop the rest of the stems; reserve. Use either individual round gratin dishes or a large dish. Grease well first with oil, then with butter.

Prepare the stuffing: Whizz together the butter, chopped mushroom stems, anchovy fillets (drained of their oil) or anchovy paste, garlic, parsley, chives, and breadcrumbs in a food processor. Using a spatula, spread the stuffing over the mushroom caps. Season lightly with salt and more generously with freshly ground black pepper. Arrange the mushrooms in the gratin dishes or dish. Bake for about 30 minutes, until the mushrooms are soft and the stuffing golden. Serve hot.

Champignons à la Poêle
Pan-Fried Mushrooms

Oyster mushrooms are called *pleurotes* in French (from the Greek word for "little ear"). Whether they look to you and me like bivalves or ears, both names are charmingly appropriate. On a recent visit to a mushroom farm near Vouvray in the Loire valley, I saw them growing commercially in a constantly lit cellar for the first time. Here they were, in fact, very mussel- rather than oysterlike, in clusters on a wall of well-insulated manure.

The owner of the place enjoyed hearing about their English name. *Très amusant, mais*... Before I could add pedantically that their French name was very apt, too, she told me just why *pleurotes* are called *pleurotes*. These mushrooms, she explained, give of their best if you cook them briefly in a little hot fat, then let them weep (*pleurer*) a while before you finish the cooking. And that, Madame, is how they got their name.

Serves 6

8 ounces (225 g) oyster
   mushrooms
1 tablespoon (15 ml) oil
4 tablespoons (60 g) butter
sea salt
1 pound (450 g) cremini
   (brown cap) mushrooms
2 or 3 cloves of garlic
several sprigs of parsley
freshly ground black pepper
1 lemon wedge, if liked
a few sprigs of chives, if liked

Heat the oil and a knob of butter in a large skillet. Break the oyster mushrooms if they look unwieldy. Sauté the oyster mushrooms over a moderately high heat for a few minutes, stirring frequently. Season with a little salt. Remove the mushrooms from the pan with a draining spoon and spread them over a double layer of paper towels. Reduce the heat and add the rest of the butter to the pan.

Trim the cremini mushrooms and cut them in half, or quarters if they are on the large side. Crush the garlic. Put the mushrooms and garlic in the pan and stir to coat in the melted butter; season with a little salt. Turn up the heat just a notch and sauté the mushrooms for several minutes, until they are nearly cooked to your liking.

Stir in the reserved oyster mushrooms. Snip in the parsley and sauté for a couple of minutes; sprinkle with a little lemon juice and snip in some chives just before serving.

Tomates Farcies Bijou
Herb-Stuffed Tomatoes

My mother's way of stuffing tomatoes—perfect if you have access to a summer garden, and also not bad with dried herbs. Particularly recommended with roast lamb and chicken dishes.

Serves 4

8 firm but ripe, medium-size tomatoes
sea salt
1 or 2 cloves of garlic
3 tablespoons (45 ml) good olive oil

2 tablespoons (30 g) breadcrumbs made from day-old bread
several sprigs each of parsley, chervil, chives, and tarragon

a few sprigs of as many of the following as you like: sweet savory, thyme, oregano, and marjoram
1 teaspoon (5 g) sugar, if liked
2 tablespoons (30 g) butter
freshly ground black pepper

Slice off the tomato tops. Using a small, sharp knife and a teaspoon, carefully remove the seeds and pulp. Sprinkle the tomatoes with a little salt. Place them upside down on paper towels and leave to drain for at least 20 minutes. Heat the oven to 350°F.

Very finely chop the garlic. Heat half the olive oil in a small saucepan and sauté the chopped garlic and breadcrumbs over a very moderate heat for a couple of minutes. Pour the sautéed garlic and breadcrumbs into a bowl. Snip in the fresh herbs, and add a teaspoon of sugar, if liked. Stir until mixed.

Using a teaspoon, fill the drained tomatoes with the herb mixture. Put a little knob of butter on the top of each filled tomato and season with freshly ground black pepper. Grease a suitable gratin dish with the rest of the oil and put in the tomatoes. Cook in the bottom of the oven for 45 minutes to 1 hour. Reduce the heat a little if the tomatoes are collapsing. Serve warm.

Pommes de Terre à la Forestière
Sautéed Potatoes with Mushrooms and Bacon

This is not so much a recipe as a way of combining two dishes to make a substantial main course.

Chop 6 slices of thickly cut unsmoked bacon. Turn to *pommes de terre sautées* on page 124. Add the chopped bacon to the rinsed and diced potatoes and follow Madame Boucher's recipe, trying not to rush the process. When the potatoes are half cooked, start preparing *champignons à la poêle*, using a sauté pan (see page 132). Combine the contents of the pans and serve with a large, sharply dressed green salad. Enough for 8.

LENTILLES AUX LARDONS
Lentils with Bacon

I LOVE LENTILS. The lentils that come from Le Puy, in the heart of the volcanic Auvergne region of central France, are the very best and worth looking for. The bacon in the dish below is a well-tried combination, but I sometimes omit it if I am in a vegetarian mood or serving the lentils as a side dish. Try this with roast chicken and, dare I say it, creamed potatoes (see page 123).

For a lighter dish, omit the onion, tomato, and bacon. Replace with a generous cup of chopped parsley, half at the beginning of cooking and the rest at the end. This version is best served *tiede*.

1½ cups (300 g) *lentilles du Puy*
  or small, dark blue-green
  lentils
1 onion
1 clove of garlic
1 large ripe tomato
2 ounces (60 g) thickly cut
  rindless smoked back bacon

Serves 4

1 tablespoon (15 ml) olive oil
2 tablespoons (30 g) butter
a few sprigs of parsley and
  thyme
1 bay leaf
sea salt
freshly ground black pepper

SOAK THE LENTILS WHILE YOU PREPARE the other ingredients. Finely chop the onion and garlic. Blanch, seed, and chop the tomato. Cut the bacon in half; chop one half into small dice.

Drain and rinse the lentils. In a large, heavy-bottomed saucepan, heat half the olive oil and a knob of butter. Add the chopped onion to the pan. Sauté over a moderate heat for a few minutes, then add the garlic and the lentils. Stir to mix with the onion and coat with the fat, then add the tomato and the unchopped half of bacon.

Add the herbs, including the bay leaf, then pour in plenty of water to completely cover the ingredients by at least 1 inch (2.5 cm).

Bring to a boil fairly slowly, then season lightly with salt and freshly ground black pepper. Cover, reduce the heat, and cook for 25 to 30 minutes, until the lentils are soft but not mushy. Lift the lid every now and then to check the cooking and add a ladleful of extra water if necessary.

When the lentils are nearly cooked, heat the rest of the oil in a small skillet. Sauté the chopped bacon over a moderate heat until crisp and golden; drain on paper towels. Drain the lentils of any excess liquid. Discard the herbs and bay leaf. Slice the piece of bacon and return to the lentils. Swirl in the rest of the butter. Sprinkle in the sautéed bacon and serve immediately.

ENDIVES AU FOUR
Baked Endive

BELGIAN ENDIVE IS A BIT of an acquired taste. As children we certainly didn't rate it much. More often than not, we used to eat endive plainly steamed, which we didn't at all like. Sometimes pan-fried with butter, which was an improvement, and less frequently, baked as below. This was a real treat, especially when the endive was wrapped in thin slices of ham before being returned to the oven for the final *gratin* stage. I now prefer this dish without ham, but then I like the slightly bitter flavor of endive a great deal more than I used to.

Serves 4

4 tablespoons (60 g) butter
1¾ pounds (800 g) Belgian
  endives (chicory)
2 teaspoons (10 g) sugar
sea salt
freshly ground black pepper
1 lemon wedge
3 tablespoons (45 ml) *crème
  fraîche* or heavy cream
1 ounce (30 g) Gruyère cheese

HEAT THE OVEN TO 350°F. SOFTEN HALF the butter. Trim and rinse the endive; discard any bruised outer leaves. Spread the softened butter over a gratin dish just large enough to take the endive in a single layer.

Arrange the endive in the dish. Sprinkle with sugar, then season lightly with salt and freshly ground black pepper. Squeeze the wedge of lemon over the endive. Dot with the rest of the butter and cover with foil.

Bake in the oven for about 30 minutes.

Grate the Gruyère into a bowl and combine with the *crème fraîche*. Season with a little black pepper. Take the dish out of the oven.

Turn up the heat to 400°F. Remove the foil, then spread the cream and cheese mixture over the endive. Return the dish to the oven and bake for 10 to 15 minutes more, until golden and sizzling. Serve hot.

DESSERTS
Desserts

WHEN I WAS A CHILD, desserts were a treat and I still think of them as such—something sweet and quite special to delight in when the occasion warrants.

My mother did not have a sweet tooth and she was concerned about *la ligne*, not so much hers, which was most elegant, but that of her three daughters who were less streamlined. The result was that we seldom ate desserts at home, twice a week at the most. The national average is probably closer to once a day.

Instead we had cheese followed by fruit. We loved the former and dutifully munched the latter—to this day I much prefer eating fruit between meals, without knife and fork. Reading recently that it is healthier to ingest fruit on its own during a meal made me feel righteous and vindicated.

Looking back on this absence of daily dessert, I am grateful for two reasons. The first is that I soon became a cheese lover, with a wealth of pleasures and interesting finds in store, not only in France, but now magnificently in Britain. The second reason is that I was spared a lot of bad and filling sweet stodge. To my mind a boring dessert simply is not worth eating.

The French think of *pâtisserie* as an art. Like other families we relied on the best local master baker and bought in elaborate cakes and ice creams. What we did at home was the object of intense discussions and comparison—after all this was no routine matter. Why did this *tarte Tatin* go wrong? Was not the *île flottante* particularly light? Perhaps there was too much orange flavoring in the chocolate cake . . . All the recipes in the shortish repertoire that follows repeatedly passed the family test.

Pommes Meringuées
Meringue Apples

A GREAT HOMELY pudding that is easy to make and likely to delight the whole family, from the very young to the very old via most reasonably self-indulging adults. I am reminded of a celebrated *Tintin* slogan that really sums up the range of family enjoyment—*pour tous les jeunnes de 7 à 77 ans*, for all the young between the ages of 7 and 77. Does conscious enjoyment start at 7 and end at 77, I sometimes wonder? I know I liked Mado's meringue apples years before I reached the Age of Reason and my grandfather, who is turning 97 at the time I am writing, still much favors them.

I tend to use Cox's apples to make this pudding—the great sharp English Bramleys tend to collapse a little too readily.

This is not a difficult dessert to make, but do not rush it and allow plenty of cooling time between the various steps, to help the moisture escape and the meringue to crisp.

The *crème pâtissière*—made with more milk than usual—is light and fairly thin.

1¾ pounds (800 g) Cox's apples
butter for greasing
7 tablespoons (110 g) superfine sugar
3 extra-large egg whites

Serves 6 to 8

FOR THE *CRÈME PÂTISSIÈRE*
3¼ cups (800 ml) milk
1 vanilla bean, split, or a few drops of vanilla extract

3 extra-large egg yolks
5 tablespoons (75 g) superfine sugar
2 heaping tablespoons (40 g) flour

MAKE THE *CRÈME PÂTISSIÈRE*. IN A SAUCEPAN, bring the milk to a boil with the split vanilla bean or a few drops of vanilla extract. Turn off the heat and, if using a vanilla bean, allow the milk to steep for 10 minutes.

Meanwhile, whisk together in a large bowl the egg yolks and sugar until the mixture is smooth and pale. Sift the flour into the egg and sugar mixture, then whisk again until well combined. Return the milk to a boil if necessary. Pour the boiling milk into the mixture and whisk until smooth and well blended.

Pour the mixture back into the pan, and bring to a boil, stirring very frequently. Keep it bubbling for at least 5 minutes, still stirring frequently, to give the flour plenty of time to cook. Leave the *crème pâtissière* to cool, giving it the occasional stir to stop a skin from forming. Heat the oven to 350°F. Peel, quarter, core, and thickly slice the apples.

Grease a large baking dish. Arrange the apple slices in the dish as evenly as possible. Sprinkle them with 1 tablespoon or so of sugar. Put the dish in the oven and cook the apples for 15 to 20 minutes—they should be just tender but not disintegrating. Remove the dish from the oven and leave the apples to cool a little. Turn the oven down to 325°F. Pour or spoon the *crème pâtissière* over the cooled apples.

Whisk the egg whites until very firm, then gradually add the sugar, a little at a time, still whisking. Spoon carefully or pipe the beaten egg whites over the *crème pâtissière*. If necessary, use a fork or the handle of a spoon to make an attractive pattern. Leave a few very tiny gaps to allow any steam to escape from the *crème pâtissière*—this will help the meringue to crisp.

Return the dish to the oven and bake for at least 20 minutes, or until the meringue is golden and crisp. Serve hot or warm.

PÊCHES AU VIN
Peaches in White Wine

PÊCHES AU VIN were a summer treat and a Fourchettes institution. In their crudest form, they were an unceremonious do-it-yourself-at-the-table concoction. While carrying on with the general conversation, you took an unpeeled peach, freshly plucked from the garden, chopped it up and tipped it into your wineglass. You then added a little wine–white, rosé, or red, depending on what you were drinking at the time, and maybe a sprinkling of sugar. As children we made a happy sugary mush in our water glasses. I can recommend the method outlined above, especially if you have a glut of bruised peaches. Steep them in lightly sugared wine and chill for an hour or so for a lovely casual dessert.

The recipe below is more formal and definitely more refined. You may like to compromise between the two.

Serves 4

4 white peaches
1¼ cups (300 ml) white wine
1 vanilla bean
3 tablespoons (45 g) sugar
2 tablespoons (30 ml)
   blackberry liqueur, *cassis* or
   red fruit liqueur

3 tablespoons (45 g) red-
   currant jelly
8 almonds, shelled and
   blanched
⅓ cup (45 g) shelled pistachios
a few mint leaves

PEEL THE PEACHES. PLUNGE THEM IN A saucepan of boiling water and keep it bubbling for a couple of minutes. Lift the peaches out of the water with a draining spoon–the peel should slip off easily. If not, boil a minute more.

Meanwhile, prepare the syrup. In a saucepan large enough to take the peaches in a single layer, combine the wine with the same quantity of water. Slit the vanilla bean in half and add to the liquid. Stir in the sugar and bring to a boil, then reduce the heat and simmer until you have peeled the peaches.

Then add the peeled peaches to the simmering liquid and gently poach for 5 minutes, turning them over carefully halfway through. Remove the peaches from the poaching liquid with a draining spoon and leave them to cool a little.

Turn up the heat and boil the liquid until reduced by half. Stir in the blackberry or other liqueur and the red-currant jelly. Carefully cut each peach in half. Remove the pits and place almonds in the cavities. Pour or spoon the syrup over the peaches.

Finely chop the shelled pistachios or, if you prefer, pound them using a mortar and pestle. Sprinkle the pistachios over the peaches and leave to macerate until cold, then chill until the dessert is needed. Arrange a mint leaf or two on top of each halved peach before serving.

Poires au Vin Rouge

Pears in Red Wine

A LATE SUMMER and fall dessert popular all over France. The prunes are a traditional Loire ingredient, sadly fast disappearing and much harder to find locally these days. For the addition of *crème de cassis* and the *broiche* suggestion I am indebted to a professional chef, my friend Ghislaine Salé of the *Auberge de la Brenne* in Neuillé Le Lierre, between Amboise and Châteaurenault. My original family recipe was somewhat more basic. Use handsome, firm pears in peak condition for this recipe.

4 ripe-but-firm Williams pears
2½ cups (600 ml) red wine
1 to 2 tablespoons (15 to 30 g)
   sugar

Serves 4

1 tablespoon (15 g) grated
   nutmeg
8 pitted prunes
2 tablespoons (30 ml) *crème de
   cassis*
little hot *brioches*, to serve, if
   liked

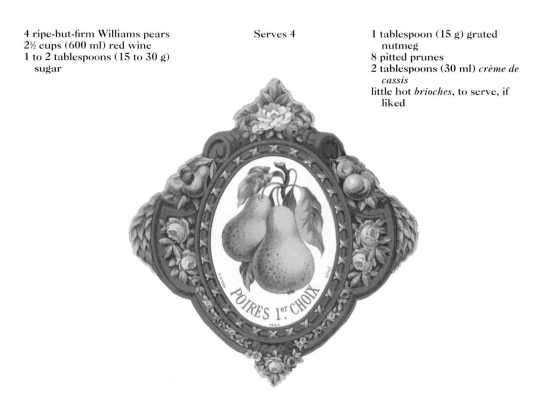

PEEL THE PEARS, KEEPING THEM WHOLE. In a heavy-bottomed saucepan large enough to hold the pears comfortably in a single layer, combine the wine, sugar, and nutmeg. Place the pears side by side in the liquid. Bring to a simmer. Add the prunes and simmer gently for about 15 minutes, until the pears are just cooked and tender.

Carefully turn the pears over once during cooking and baste occasionally with the simmering wine.

Using a draining spoon, remove the pears and prunes from the liquid. Leave to cool on a serving dish or in individual coupes; the pears look best upright.

Turn up the heat, add the *crème de cassis* to the wine, and boil until the liquid becomes a little syrupy and is reduced by half. Spoon or pour the syrup over the pears and prunes and serve *tiède* or chilled. If you are serving the pears *tièdes*, hot *brioches* make a splendid accompaniment.

COMPOTE D'ABRICOTS ET DE FRAISES
Apricot and Strawberry Compote

THE TRICK WITH COMPOTES is not to allow the fruit to collapse into a purée. I like the combination below very much. It tastes even better if the raw strawberries you add at the end are *fraises des bois*, wild strawberries.

¾ cup (150 g) sugar
1 vanilla bean
1½ pounds (750 g) ripe firm
   apricots

Serves 6

12 ounces (350 g) ripe
   strawberries
½ lemon

IN A SAUCEPAN, COMBINE 1¼ CUPS (300 ML) water with the sugar. Split the vanilla bean and add to the liquid. Bring to a boil, then simmer while you halve and pit the apricots. Add the halved apricots to the simmering liquid and continue to simmer for 8 to 10 minutes. Meanwhile, rinse the strawberries under cold running water, then hull them.

Remove the apricots from the pan with a draining spoon and place in a bowl. Turn up the heat and bring the syrup to a boil.

Reduce it a little, then add half the strawberries. Turn down the heat, and cook very gently for a few minutes. Remove the vanilla bean (dry and keep to use again), then add the poached strawberries and the syrup to the apricots. Stir, very gently, to mix.

Squeeze the lemon and, if they are very large, halve the rest of the strawberries. Add to the compote, sprinkle with the lemon juice, and very gently stir the mixture. Refrigerate for at least 1 hour. Serve chilled.

CRÈME ANGLAISE
Custard

A GREAT ALL-A-ROUNDER that can be flavored with a dash of strong black coffee, grated orange or lemon zest, liqueur, or rum. *Crème anglaise* is very flexible; the quantities below are average. For a thicker, sweeter cream to serve, for example, with a sharp fruit purée or compote, use less milk (2 cups/450 ml) and more sugar (generous ½ cup/120 g).

2 vanilla beans, or a few drops
   of vanilla extract
2½ cups (600 ml) milk

Serves 4

3 extra-large or large egg yolks
6 tablespoons (90 g) superfine
   sugar

IF YOU ARE USING VANILLA BEANS, SPLIT them in half lengthwise. Bring the milk to a boil with the vanilla flavoring. Turn off the heat and leave to cool. Meanwhile, in a separate saucepan, whisk together the egg yolks and sugar until smooth and pale.

Remove the vanilla beans, if using. Over a very low heat, pour the warm milk, a little at a time, into the egg yolk and sugar

mixture, stirring well. Bring the mixture almost, but not quite, to a boiling point very slowly, stirring constantly with a large wooden spoon. Do not let it boil and take it off the heat occasionally while it is cooking.

Once the cream is cooked and thickened so it coats the back of the wooden spoon, strain it through a fine strainer. If you are serving it cold, stir occasionally as it cools.

ŒUFS À LA NEIGE
Eggs in the Snow

THIS IS A FAVORITE PARTY DISH—light as a feather, festive looking, and, last but not least, economical. Another advantage of *œufs à la neige* is that they can be prepared a day or two ahead, and taste all the better for it.

3¾ cups (900 ml) milk
1½ cups (300 g) superfine sugar
2 vanilla beans
5 extra-large eggs
6 sugared almonds

Serves 4 to 6

FOR THE CARAMEL
6 tablespoons (90 g) superfine sugar

BRING THE MILK TO A BOIL IN A LARGE saucepan with half the sugar and the split vanilla beans. Keep an eye on the milk while it is coming to a boil. Separate the eggs; reserve the yolks. Whisk the whites until they begin to stiffen, then sprinkle in 2 tablespoons of sugar and whisk the mixture until very firm.

Lower the heat. Remove the vanilla beans from the milk, then scoop up 4 big spoonfuls of whisked egg white and poach them very gently in the simmering milk, for just over 1 minute on each side, flipping them over carefully. Remove the egg "meringues" from the milk, drain well, and reserve on a clean cloth. Repeat the process until you have used up all the whisked egg white, making sure the milk never gets back up to boiling point.

Strain the milk. In a saucepan, beat the reserved egg yolks with the rest of the sugar until smooth and much paler in color. Turn down the heat to very low. Pour the hot milk a little at a time into the egg yolk mixture, stirring constantly with a wooden spoon, and cook very slowly until the cream begins to thicken. Never allow the mixture to boil. Take the pan off the heat occasionally and continue stirring until the cream is just thick enough to coat the back of the wooden spoon. Remove from the heat and leave the cream to cool completely, stirring it occasionally.

Pour the cooled cream into a large glass bowl and carefully arrange the cooked egg whites on top—they will float.

Prepare the caramel. In a medium-size saucepan, combine the sugar with 6 tablespoons (90 ml) water, stirring until dissolved, then bring to a boil and continue boiling without stirring until you have a thick, rich brown syrup. Immediately trickle this sticky caramel syrup over the egg whites.

Roughly crush the sugared almonds—I use a mortar and pestle or the small bowl of my food processor—and sprinkle them over the dish. Refrigerate overnight and serve very cold.

ILE FLOTTANTE
Floating Island

ANOTHER FLUFFY AND hard-to-resist egg dessert that can be prepared well in advance. I believe that *île flottante* once described as a layered cake of *brioche* or sponge, apricot marmalade, almonds, and dried raisins set on a custard or red fruit purée, but I have never personally encountered the old-style pudding.

3 extra-large or 4 large egg whites
heaping ½ cup (120 g) superfine sugar
9 sugared almonds or 2 small dry macaroons

Serves 4 to 6

FOR THE CARAMEL
heaping ⅓ cup (75 g) superfine sugar, or light brown sugar

TO SERVE
crème anglaise (see page 140) or red fruit purée (see opposite)

MAKE THE CARAMEL. IN A SMALL SAUCEPAN, combine the sugar with 5 to 6 tablespoons of water. Stir until dissolved over a gentle heat, then turn up the heat and boil without stirring until the syrup turns golden brown. Pour at once into a *moule à manqué*, ring mold, or charlotte mold and swirl to coat all over.

Coarsely crush the sugared almonds or macaroons using a mortar and pestle. Heat the oven to 325°F. Whisk the egg whites until firm, then gradually mix in the sugar and crushed sugared almonds or macaroons. Continue whisking until the meringue mixture is stiff.

Bring a full kettle of water to a boil. Line the bottom of a large roasting pan with several layers of newspaper. Pour the meringue mixture into the prepared mold. Put the mold in the center of the lined roasting pan. Pour in boiling water to come halfway up the sides of the mold. Cook the meringue in this *bain-marie* for about 40 minutes, keeping an eye on the level of the water; pour in extra boiling water if necessary.

Leave the floating island to cool completely before unmolding it onto a serving dish.

Serve chilled, over *crème anglaise* or red fruit purée. If using red fruit purée, stir into it the juice of a lemon and sweeten to taste with confectioners' sugar rather than using superfine sugar.

Glace Double à la Vanille et aux Fruits Rouges

Vanilla and Red Fruit Ice Cream

This is a good ice cream for the berry season. Use the egg whites to make meringues.

1¼-pound (600-g) mixture of
   some, or all, of the following:
   strawberries, raspberries,
   blackberries, red currants
¾ cup (150 g) superfine sugar
2½ cups (600 ml) heavy cream
strawberries and raspberries,
   to serve, if liked

Serves 8 to 10

FOR THE *CRÈME ANGLAISE*
1½ cups (350 ml) full-fat milk
3 vanilla beans or several
   drops of vanilla extract
4 large egg yolks
heaping ½ cup (120 g) superfine
   sugar

Make a thick *crème anglaise* (see page 140), strain it through a fine strainer or *chinois* and whisk it frequently while it gets cold. Rinse and clean the fruit. Purée in the food processor, then press the purée through a strainer into a bowl. Stir the sugar into the fruit purée until absorbed.

Whip the thick cream until firm. Reserve about one-third of the whipped cream and carefully fold the rest into the fruit purée. Pour or spoon the fruit and cream mixture into a tray and freeze.

Fold the reserved whipped cream into the cold custard. Flavor with a little extra vanilla extract if you like. Pour the mixture into a second tray of the same size as the first tray and freeze. After 30 to 40 minutes, remove both iced preparations from the freezer and stir to prevent ice crystals from forming. Repeat the process twice, then leave until completely frozen—the vanilla ice cream is less likely to crystallize than the other.

Remove the trays from the freezer about 10 minutes before serving and serve the vanilla ice cream on top of the red fruit ice cream in a serving dish. If you like, surround the ice-cream sandwich with extra strawberries and raspberries.

CERISES LÉGISLATIVES
Cherry Ring

A JOLLY WAY TO enhance plain vanilla ice cream, bearing a jokey title which, for the French, has republican or even revolutionary overtones.

1 pound (450 g) sweet ripe cherries
2½ tablespoons (40 g) unsalted butter

Serves 4 to 6

4 tablespoons (60 g) superfine sugar

the juice of 1 large orange
the juice of 1 large lemon
2 tablespoons (30 ml) kirsh
2 tablespoons (30 ml) *crème de cassis*
vanilla ice cream, to serve

RINSE THE CHERRIES AND REMOVE THE stems and pits. In a heavy-bottomed saucepan, melt the butter over a low heat.

Add the stoned cherries, sugar, and orange and lemon juices and simmer gently for 5 to 10 minutes, stirring delicately every now and then.

Drain the cherries over a bowl. Reserve the cherries and return the poaching juices to the pan. Bring to a simmer and reduce by about one-third.

Add the kirsh and *crème de cassis*, then bring to a boil, and bubble for 2 to 3 minutes.

Meanwhile, arrange the cherries around piled-up scoops of vanilla ice cream. If you are serving this dessert in individual cups, allow 3 scoops per person. Spoon the sauce over the ice cream and serve immediately.

GÂTEAU À L'ORANGE
Orange Cake

ANOTHER RECIPE FROM MY aunt Yonnée, which brings back hazy memories of my grandmother, mother, and aunts rather reluctantly hosting a ladies' tea. For that old-fashioned institution, *le goûter de dames*, the finest china came out and best behavior was *de rigueur*. We all watched from a safe distance.

heaping ½ cup (125 g) superfine sugar
6 tablespoons (90 g) soft unsalted butter, plus extra for greasing
2 extra-large eggs

Serves 6

⅔ cup (125 g) self-rising flour
1 scant teaspoon (4 g) baking powder
1 large juicy orange
1 tablespoon (15 ml) Cointreau

FOR THE GLAZING
5 tablespoons (75 ml) orange juice
1 tablespoon (15 ml) Cointreau
7 to 8 tablespoons (110 to 125 g) confectioners' sugar

HEAT THE OVEN TO 350°F. BEAT THE SUGAR and butter together until creamy. Beat in the eggs. Sift the flour and baking powder over the mixture and fold them in lightly.

Grate the zest of the orange and squeeze out the juice. Stir zest, juice, and Cointreau into the batter. Then grease a 5-cup (1.2-liter) bread pan and spoon in the batter. Knock the pan against the countertop to settle the contents. Bake for about 50 minutes, until the cake is firm but bouncy to the touch and the blade of a knife inserted into it comes out clean. Leave it to cool for 10 to 15 minutes, then unmold onto a dish.

Meanwhile, prepare the glazing. In a small saucepan, gently warm the orange juice and Cointreau. Stir in the confectioners' sugar.

Using a pastry brush, paint the glaze over the cake—some of the glaze will seep in, the rest will form a light crust. Serve cold.

Gâteau Glacé au Moka
Iced Mocha Gâteau

Hard to resist. I tend to prefer this grown-up dessert without the optional extras, but candied angelica and cherries make fine additions.

7 ounces (200 g) bittersweet
   chocolate
2 tablespoons (30 g) good-
   quality instant coffee
   granules
1 cup (200 g) superfine sugar
14 tablespoons (200 g) unsalted
   butter, plus extra for
   greasing
5 large eggs

Serves 6 to 8

sea salt
6 tablespoons (90 ml) brandy
3 tablespoons (45 ml) kirsch
27 to 30 *biscuits à la cuiller* or
   36 ladyfingers

To serve (optional)
candied mixed fruit
candied cherries

Break the chocolate into small pieces and place in a heavy-bottomed saucepan with ½ cup (120 ml) boiling water. Leave to stand for 3 minutes, then pour out the water and stir the chocolate over a very low heat until creamy.

Stir in the coffee granules, then set aside the pan over a bowl of boiling water, giving this cream an occasional stir.

Meanwhile, whisk together the sugar and butter until pale golden and foamy.

Separate the eggs, one at a time, collecting the whites in a large bowl and whisking each yolk into the sugar and butter. Whisk the mixture well after adding each yolk.

When all the yolks have been incorporated, whisk in the chocolate and coffee cream, a little at a time. If it feels too thick and solid, beat in a tablespoon or two of hot water before adding to the butter, sugar, and yolk mixture.

Add a pinch of salt to the egg whites and whisk until stiff. Now fold the whisked egg whites into the chocolate mixture, using a large metal spoon or balloon whisk, which-

ever you are most comfortable with. Start by folding in a couple of spoonfuls, then tip in the rest. The important thing is to work lightly and with upward movements to get air into the mixture. Stop working as soon as the egg whites are absorbed.

Generously butter a large 12½-cup (2.5-liter) bread pan.

Combine the brandy and kirsch with 3 tablespoons water in a soup plate. Quickly dip each cookie into this mixture and line the bottom of the bread pan with a layer of cookies; continue with a second layer of cookies.

Spoon in the chocolate and coffee mousse. Knock the pan once or twice against the countertop to settle the contents. Cover with 2 layers of cookies soaked in the brandy mixture.

Freeze overnight or for several hours, making sure the freezer is not turned to the highest/coldest setting.

Remove the iced gâteau from the freezer a few minutes before serving. Turn out onto a long platter. If you like, arrange pieces of candied fruit around the gâteau.

TARTE AU CITRON
Lemon Tart

THIS IS MY VERSION of my sister Françoise's recipe, which she jotted down a long time ago at our cousin Florence's . . . It is sharp, zesty, and a most pleasing way to round off a meal.

Serves 6

FOR THE TART CRUST
10 tablespoons (150 g) unsalted butter, plus extra for greasing
1 extra-large egg
⅓ cup (75 g) superfine sugar
a small pinch of salt

1¾ cups (250 g) flour, plus extra for flouring

FOR THE FILLING
8 tablespoons (120 g) unsalted butter

1 cup (200 g) superfine sugar
1 unwaxed orange
3 unwaxed juicy lemons
3 extra-large or 5 large eggs

LEAVE THE BUTTER IN A WARM PLACE until softened. Prepare the tart crust. In a bowl, whisk the egg with the sugar and a small pinch of salt until the mixture is light and foamy. Sift the flour into a second bowl, then tip it all at once into the egg and sugar mixture. Work the mixture lightly with your fingertips until it begins to feel like coarse sand. Cut the softened butter into small pieces and work into the mixture until the dough is smooth. Roll the dough into a ball and refrigerate for at least 1 hour.

Heat the oven to 350°F. Dust a rolling pin with flour and generously grease a tart pan with butter. Roll out the dough and line the prepared pan—I invariably end up using my hands to flatten the dough and fit it into the pan, as it is very "short," breaking easily.

Now make the filling. Combine the softened butter with the sugar, beating vigorously until the mixture is smooth.

Finely grate the orange and 1 or 2 lemons—the more zest you use, the sharper and more lemony the filling. Squeeze all the lemons. Whisk the eggs a little longer than you would for an omelet. Stir the grated zests and the lemon juice into the butter and sugar mixture. Whisk in the beaten eggs.

Pour the filling into the prepared dough case and bake for 35 to 40 minutes, until the filling is set and the crust cooked. Cool before you remove the tart from the pan.

TATIN EXPRESS
Quick Upside-Down Apple Tart

NOT THE REAL THING, but very good indeed if you are pushed for time. The shortcut idea came from my cousin Isabelle, who is a great believer in never spending more than a few minutes at a time in her kitchen.

Serves 6

1½ pounds (750 g) crisp eating apples
4 tablespoons (60 g) soft unsalted butter, plus extra to finish

6 tablespoons (90 g) superfine sugar, plus extra to finish
8 ounces (225 g) store-bought piecrust dough, rolled out slightly larger than the pan

HEAT THE OVEN AND A LARGE BAKING sheet to 400°F. Very generously grease the base and sides of a loose-bottomed tart pan. Sprinkle liberally with sugar. Quarter and core the apples, then arrange them evenly and tightly in the prepared pan. Sprinkle the apples with the rest of the sugar and dot with the rest of the butter. Place the sheet of prepared dough over the apples. Trim and fit it in all around between the apples and the sides of the pan.

Place the pan on the hot baking sheet and bake for 20 to 25 minutes, until the pastry is cooked and golden. Check after 10 or 15 minutes and lower the heat if the pastry is browning too quickly.

Remove the pan from the oven and let it cool for a good 15 minutes. When it is cool enough to handle comfortably, cover the pan with a serving dish, then carefully turn both pan and dish upside down. Now remove the ring and bottom, easing them off the tart with a knife if necessary. Dot the tart with a little extra butter and sprinkle it with a little more sugar. Pop it under a hot broiler until the butter and sugar bubble. Serve warm.

TARTE TATIN
Caramelized Upside-Down Apple Tart

A WONDERFUL, BUT tricky, dish, with an infuriating tendency either to burn or not to caramelize enough. You can make a *Tatin* in a deep flameproof tart pan, but it helps enormously if you use the proper French pan, a *moule à manqué*, which is round and about 2 inches (5 cm) deep. I have just invested in a heavy-bottomed stainless-steel mold that conveniently comes with its own serving dish. A good kitchen equipment store should be able to supply you with a *moule à manqué*.

I would love to take part in a *Tatin* workshop–every cook who "does" this dessert seems to have a different recipe. The method below is the one I am happiest with at the moment. I add "at the moment" because it is likely to evolve: The sprinkling of sugar over the pastry is something I have only just started doing. To give credit where it is due, let me explain that it is a little *truc* my sister Anne-Sophie kindly let me in to the last time I congratulated her on the crispness of her *Tatin* pastry.

Serves 6 to 8

2½ pounds (1.2 kg) crisp eating apples, such as Cox's	FOR THE TART CRUST 1½ cups (225 g) flour	2 tablespoons (30 ml) *crème fraîche* or sour cream
8 tablespoons (120 g) soft unsalted butter	1 tablespoon (15 g) superfine sugar, plus extra to sprinkle	
¾ cup (150 g) superfine sugar	a small pinch of salt	TO SERVE (OPTIONAL) Calvados
	10 tablespoons (150 g) soft unsalted butter	*crème fraîche* or sour cream

PREPARE THE DOUGH. SIFT THE FLOUR into a bowl, add the sugar and salt, and stir to combine. Cut the butter into small pieces, then work it into the flour with your fingertips. Once the butter has been absorbed, work in the *crème fraîche*. Roll into a ball, wrap in plastic wrap, and chill for at least half an hour.

Melt half the butter in the pan. Remove from the heat. Sprinkle half the sugar over the melted butter and swirl to mix; make sure that the edge of the pan is well coated with butter and sugar.

Peel and core the apples. Cut them in half, which is traditional, or into chunky quarters, which I prefer. Arrange the apples over the butter and sugar, packing them in tightly. Sprinkle them with the rest of the sugar and dot with the rest of the butter.

Place on top of the stove over a moderately high heat for 10 to 15 minutes, until the butter and sugar look golden and lightly caramelized; keep a sharp eye on it to make sure the mixture does not turn too brown. Remove the pan from the heat, and leave until just cool enough to handle. Heat the oven to 425°F.

Lightly dust a rolling pin with flour and roll out the dough, not too thinly. Make sure that your circle of dough is 2 inches (5 cm) larger than the pan. You may need to use your hands as well–this dough tends to crumble. Place the rolled out dough over the apples. Using your fingers, tuck it in well between the apples and the edge of the pan. Sprinkle a little sugar over the surface to make it more crunchy and prick in several places with a fork. Bake in the oven for about 30 minutes, until the pastry is golden.

Remove from the oven, and leave to cool for a few minutes. Cover with a serving dish slightly larger than the pan you have used. *Tarte Tatin* is best served barely warm. Turn over and unmold onto the dish just before serving, knocking the serving dish against the countertop and tapping the tin sharply.

Rearrange the apples a little if necessary. Serve the *tarte* on its own, or sprinkled with Calvados and/or accompanied by a small bowl of *crème fraîche*, as you wish.

Petits Soufflés Fondants au Chocolat au Coulis de Framboises

Soft-Centered Chocolate Soufflés with Raspberry Sauce

When in doubt, I serve a hot chocolate dessert. Over the years I have tried a number of individual chocolate soufflés and chef-style fondants. This is the most fun to prepare and delicious to eat. Very conveniently, you can freeze the mixture in the ramekins, then bake from frozen for 20 minutes. Don't leave in the oven longer than instructed–the center has to be runny. You can't go wrong, but I have to warn you that the texture is delightfully unpredictable. One of my "students" called me the day after a demonstration to breezily ask if it was a safe dish to do. She was having 12 people to dinner. There was no time for a practice run. If you feel timid, don't turn the soufflés out the first time you try them. But resist the temptation to overcook: Better a very runny fondant in a ramekin than a harder cake on a plate.

2½ ounces (75 g) soft unsalted butter, plus extra for greasing
1 ounce (30 g) unsweetened cocoa powder, plus extra for dusting
6 ounces (175 g) top-quality bittersweet chocolate

Serves 6

¾ ounce (20 g) self-rising flour
1½ tablespoons (22 ml) B&B (Benedictine and brandy), or 2 teaspoons (10 ml) each brandy and Cointreau
3 fresh eggs
6 ounces (175 g) superfine sugar

Raspberry coulis for serving
14 ounces (400 g) raspberries, fresh or frozen and defrosted
confectioners' sugar to taste
1 tablespoon (15 ml) lemon juice

Grease 6 individual 4-inch (10-cm) ramekins. Dust with cocoa powder and chill for at least 1 hour.

Make the raspberry coulis. Blast the raspberries in a blender or food processor until puréed. Push through a strainer, then rinse out the bowl of the blender or processor with 6 tablespoons of water. Add to the strainer and push through. Sweeten to taste with confectioners' sugar, stir, and add the lemon juice. Chill until needed.

Heat the oven to 375°F. Place a bowl over a saucepan of simmering water, making sure there is space between the bottom of the bowl and the water. Break the chocolate into small pieces. Place in the bowl with the butter and leave to melt.

Separate the eggs. Put the whites into a large bowl, preferably copper or metal. In a second smaller bowl, lightly beat the yolks as for an omelet.

Tip the sugar into a small saucepan, add 5 tablespoons water. Place over a moderate heat and leave to bubble gently until you have a pale golden syrup.

Meanwhile, whisk the eggs until they stiffen into a meringue. Still whisking, trickle the syrup into the meringue. Whisk until well blended in; set aside.

Mix the flour and cocoa powder. Take the melted chocolate off the heat, and sift in the flour and cocoa mixture. Leave to cool a little, whisk in the egg yolks, whisking until smooth. Gently fold the chocolate mixture into the meringue. Then spoon the mixture into the prepared ramekins, and tap them against the countertop to make sure there are not any air bubbles. Bake for 15 minutes (20 if frozen) and no longer.

Invert the contents of the ramekins onto plates before serving. Add a trickle of raspberry coulis, and dust with extra cocoa powder.

Mousse au Chocolat
Chocolate Mousse

Too many nasty concoctions go under the name of chocolate mousse–mean little messes of chocolaty *ersatz* and gluey gelatin, in small plastic tubs or large institutional bowls. To my mind chocolate mousse belongs in the home. All you need is good-quality semisweet chocolate, eggs, unsalted butter, a little sugar, and maybe a dash of spirits. You can then concoct a generous dessert that few will resist. A proper chocolate mousse should be deep brown, glossy, and close textured. Not a particle of gelatin in sight, just lashings of chocolate held together smoothly by the eggs and butter.

I like to flavor the chocolate with Cointreau, but whiskey, rum, or brandy also work well.

5 ounces (150 g) best
  semisweet chocolate
4 tablespoons (60 g) soft
  unsalted butter

Serves 5 or 6

2 eggs, at room temperature

3 egg whites, at room
  temperature
1 to 2 tablespoons (15 to 30 g)
  superfine sugar
a dash of Cointreau (optional)

Break the chocolate into small pieces. Grease a saucepan with a little of the butter, then melt the chocolate completely over a very low heat, stirring occasionally with a wooden spoon; keep the heat very low throughout. As soon as the chocolate melts, remove the pan from the heat and stir in the rest of the butter until it completely melts.

Carefully break the eggs, putting the whites into a large bowl and making sure they are entirely free of yolk. Gently stir the yolks into the chocolate mixture until they are thoroughly absorbed, then leave to cool. When the mixture is almost at room temperature, whisk the egg whites until thick and foamy. Add the sugar and whisk until stiff and slightly glossy peaks form.

Using a large metal spoon or balloon whisk, fold a spoonful of whisked egg white into the chocolate mixture; mix it in well. Stir in a dash of Cointreau, if liked. Fold in the rest with a metal spoon or balloon whisk. The important thing is to work lightly with upward movements to get as much air as possible into the mixture. Stop working as soon as the egg whites are completely absorbed.

Pour the mousse into a serving dish, stemmed glasses, or ramekins and refrigerate overnight, or for at least 3 hours.

CHARLOTTE AUX AMANDES ET AUX PISTACHES
Almond and Pistachio Charlotte

THE FACT THAT charlottes were probably a tribute to King George III's wife and could therefore be regarded as an English dessert is largely forgotten in France, where they are a popular family dessert. The word is used very loosely, but charlottes tend to be a mousse, *bavaroise*, or bombe mixture encased in cookies soaked in liqueur or coffee and chilled in a deep, round mold, wider at the top than at the bottom. The recipe below impressed many a dinner-party guest at my parents' table, served on a fine white china-stemmed dish with a pale green and gold rim. I used to think that the green of the dish matching the pistachios was the height of refinement. With the considerable amount of kirsch absorbed by the cookies, this is no nursery dessert but, on charlotte nights, we always stayed awake until we could hear the guests and our parents safely ensconced back in the sitting room after dinner. The nutty, boozy, exciting leftovers were then ours to feast on like sleepy vultures. This winner of a dessert is very conveniently made the day before the party.

Serves 6 to 8

20 to 24 *biscuits à la cuiller,* or about 30 ladyfingers
kirsch
1 heaping cup (225 g) superfine sugar, plus a little extra to sweeten the water
1 extra-large egg
2¼ sticks (250 g) soft unsalted butter

2½ cups (250 g) finely ground blanched almonds
¾ cup (90 g) shelled pistachio nuts, grated
crème anglaise (see page 140), to serve

SOAK THE COOKIES OR LADYFINGERS IN A mixture of kirsch and water sweetened with sugar. Line the bottom of a 4½-cup (1.1-liter) charlotte mold with cookies, trimming them to shape, flat sides facing up. Then line the side of the mold with overlapping cookies or ladyfingers, flat sides facing in.

Cream together the sugar, egg, and butter until totally combined and smooth, then work in the ground almonds and half the grated pistachios. Flavor the mixture with kirsch and spoon it into the lined charlotte mold. Cover with soaked cookies or lady-fingers. Top with a plate. Place a weight on the plate and chill overnight in the refrigerator. Keep the remaining pistachios wrapped in plastic wrap in the refrigerator as well.

To serve, carefully unmold the charlotte onto a serving plate; do not worry if some of the cookies get a little damaged in the process. Pour some cold *crème anglaise* over it, thus concealing minor disasters, and spoon more *crème anglaise* around the bottom of the charlotte. Sprinkle with the rest of the pistachios.

PROFITEROLES AU CHOCOLAT
Chocolate Profiteroles

MADO'S PROFITEROLES WERE absolutely top of the family pops, requested with amazing regularity for birthdays and other high days. *Crème pâtissière* is the more traditional filling, but we all loved vanilla ice cream. When I make this dessert these days, I use good-quality store-bought ice cream rather than make my own. *Paresseuse*–you lazy girl, said Mado, the last time we discussed the dish on the phone.

FOR THE CHOUX
8 tablespoons (120 g) unsalted
    butter
1 cup (150 g) flour
1 cup (250 ml) water
salt
3 extra-large or 4 large eggs
dash of milk for glazing

Serves 6

FOR THE FILLING
vanilla ice cream or thick
    crème pâtissière, made as on
    page 137, but using only
    1¼ cups (300 ml) milk

FOR THE CHOCOLATE SAUCE
4 ounces (120 g) bittersweet
    chocolate
2 tablespoons (30 g) superfine
    sugar
2 tablespoons (30 g) heavy
    cream
2 tablespoons (30 g) unsalted
    butter

CUT THE BUTTER INTO DICE. SIFT THE flour on a sheet of wax paper. In a heavy-bottomed saucepan, bring the water to a boil with the diced butter and a very small pinch of salt. As soon as the liquid begins to boil, remove the pan from the heat. Quickly and all at once add the flour and immediately start stirring it in with a spatula or wooden spoon. Return to the heat and continue to stir briskly until the paste comes off the pan and looks smooth and a little shiny.

Remove from the heat and stir for 1 minute more. Add the eggs one at a time, mixing them in vigorously until the paste comes together again. Beat the last egg before you add it in, since you may need only a fraction of it; you should end up with a glossy, floppy paste, not a runny, liquid one. Continue beating for a couple of minutes to give the paste more body.

Heat the oven to 375°F. Grease a baking sheet. Fit a pastry bag with a plain ½-inch (0.5-cm) tip and spoon the paste into the bag. Pipe the paste onto the baking sheet, shaping it into balls, about the size of a small tomato. Keep them at least 1½ inches (4 cm) apart. If you do not like using a pastry bag, use a tablespoon instead–the end result will just look a little rougher. Brush the paste lightly with any remaining egg yolk mixed with a dash of milk.

Bake for about 30 minutes, until well risen and brown. Leave to stand 5 minutes in the oven before taking out, to dry the puffs a little. Slit the warm puffs sideways, almost but not quite in half, but wait until they are cold before you fill them.

If you are using *crème pâtissière*, you can fill the choux well ahead of serving. Spoon in a little of the *crème pâtissière* and keep in a cool place.

Break the chocolate into small pieces. Place the pieces in a saucepan with ½ cup (120 ml) water and the sugar. Melt over a very low heat, stirring frequently with a wooden spoon. When the mixture is smooth, stir in the cream. Take the pan off the heat and swirl in the butter, stirring until it is melted, to give the sauce a nice gloss.

If you are intending to fill the choux puffs with vanilla ice cream, do so after taking the chocolate sauce off the heat. Quickly spoon in the ice cream.

Pile the filled choux on a dish–they look much more attractive this way than in individual coupes. Pour over some of the chocolate sauce and serve the rest in a sauceboat.

LE GÂTEAU AU CHOCOLAT
Chocolate Cake

MY IDEA OF what a homemade chocolate cake should be: dark, rich, solid, irresistible, and definitely for feast days. Over the years I have played with other ideas, but I always loyally come back to this recipe. In my experience this cake disappears pretty quickly, but it will keep nicely moist for several days in the refrigerator, wrapped loosely in foil. It also travels well and will make you a popular weekend or party guest–but leave making the coating until you have arrived with your gift. The coating is over the top, and optional–but highly recommended.

	Serves 8	FOR THE COATING (OPTIONAL)
7 ounces (200 g) good-quality bittersweet chocolate		7 ounces (200 g) good-quality bittersweet chocolate
¾ cup (150 g) superfine sugar	5 large eggs	7 ounces (200 ml) light cream
12 tablespoons (175 g) soft unsalted butter, plus extra for greasing	a small pinch of salt	4 walnuts, if liked
3 heaping tablespoons (60 g) self-rising flour	grated zest of 1 small orange, or a dash of Cointreau, to flavor, if liked	

BREAK THE CHOCOLATE INTO SMALL PIECES. In a large, heavy-bottomed saucepan, melt the chocolate pieces with 2 tablespoons of water over an extremely low heat, stirring frequently with a wooden spoon. Stir in the sugar and take the pan off the heat while you cut the butter.

Return the pan to a very low heat and stir in the butter, a little at a time. Now sift in the flour, stir lightly to combine and cook for a couple of minutes, still over a low heat. Remove the pan from the heat and let the mixture cool a little.

Meanwhile, heat the oven to 325°F, and generously grease a 2¾-quart (2.5-liter) bread or cake pan.

Separate the eggs: the whites can be collected together in a large bowl, but the yolks should be put on individual saucers– or an oyster plate with its "scoops" is helpful here. Work the yolks into the chocolate mixture, one at a time, beating them in thoroughly. Add a pinch of salt to the egg whites and whisk until very firm and stiff.

Using a large metal spoon, fold the whisked egg whites into the chocolate mixture very thoroughly, but working lightly and with upward movements. If you like, flavor with the grated zest of a small orange or a dash of Cointreau. Tip the batter into the greased pan and knock the pan on the countertop a couple of times to make sure the batter is evenly settled.

Bake for about 45 minutes. Resist opening the oven door for the first 25 minutes, then check and turn the pan around if the cake is looking lopsided. Turn up the heat to the next setting for the last 5 minutes–insert a knife into the cake to check that it is baked:; the blade should come out clean and dry. Leave to cool for 15 minutes, then carefully remove the cake from the pan and place it on a serving dish.

If you decide to coat the cake, wait until it is cold. Break the chocolate into small pieces and melt it with the cream in a saucepan over a very low heat, stirring frequently with a wooden spoon. Leave the mixture to cool a little, then pour it over the center of the cake. Have a soft spatula at hand to smooth the coating evenly over the whole surface. Shell the walnuts and arrange them over the cake, if desired.

Gâteau aux Noix
Walnut Cake

THE FRESHER THE WALNUTS, the better this cake will taste. It begs to be served with a cup of properly made coffee, but I once enjoyed it with a very vinous glass of mature Cahors.

9 ounces (250 g) fresh walnuts
3 large eggs
1 heaping cup (225 g) superfine sugar
⅓ cup (60 g) self-rising flour, plus extra for flouring

Serves 6

1 tablespoon (15 ml) rum
butter for greasing

FOR THE COATING
3 ounces (90 g) bittersweet chocolate
3 tablespoons (45 ml) light cream
2 tablespoons (30 g) unsalted butter

HEAT THE OVEN TO 350°F. FINELY CHOP or pound the walnuts, reserving 9 attractive pieces. Separate the eggs. In a bowl, whisk together the sugar and egg yolks until smooth and pale. Stir in the chopped walnuts, then sift in the flour and sprinkle in the rum. Whisk lightly to combine.

In a separate bowl, whisk the egg whites until stiff, then delicately fold them into the mixture, using a large metal spoon. Work them in lightly, with upward movements, until absorbed.

Grease and flour a *moule à manqué* or deep tart pan. Pour the mixture into the prepared pan, knock the pan once or twice against the countertop to settle the contents. Bake the cake for 40 minutes, until it is firm to the touch. Leave to cool for a few minutes, then turn it onto a rack and leave until cold.

To make the coating, break the chocolate into small pieces. In a saucepan, combine the chocolate with 3 tablespoons of water and the cream. Heat slowly over a very low heat, stirring constantly with a wooden spoon, until the mixture is smooth. Take the pan off the heat and stir in the butter. Pour the coating over the center of the cake and spread with a soft spatula. Arrange the reserved walnut pieces at regular intervals around the cake, and place one in the center.

Quatre-Quarts
French Pound Cake

LITERALLY MEANING FOUR QUARTERS—equal weights of egg, butter, sugar, and flour—the French pound cake is a great standby, often served as a family dessert with stewed fruit compote (see page 140), fruit salad, or, midafternoon, with a cup of tea (a more popular beverage in France than rumor would have it). Lemon, vanilla, and orange are all traditional discreet flavorings. The ground almonds are a family addition.

2 extra-large or 3 large eggs
¾ cup (150 g) superfine sugar
finely grated zest of 1 lemon or
  orange, or a little vanilla
  extract
10 tablespoons (150 g) soft
  unsalted butter

Serves 4 to 6

1 cup (150 g) self-rising flour,
  plus extra for dusting
2 heaping tablespoons (40 g)
  finely ground blanched
  almonds

HEAT THE OVEN TO 350°F. BEAT THE eggs, sugar, and flavoring together until pale and a little frothy. Pour the butter in a bread pan or deep round *moule à manquè* pan and heat it in the oven until almost melted. Swirl to coat the pan lightly with butter, then pour the melted butter into the egg mixture a little at a time, whisking until thoroughly blended. Sift the flour over the egg and sugar mixture, a little at a time, then fold it in gently with a large metal spoon. Now fold in the ground almonds.

Dust the pan with a little flour, pour in the batter, and bake for 30 to 35 minutes. If the top browns too quickly, cover it with a piece of foil. To check that the cake is cooked, insert a skewer. When the cake is done you will find that the skewer comes out clean and dry.

Turn out the cake onto a rack as soon as it comes out of the oven and leave to get cold before serving.

The cake will keep well for a few days wrapped in foil and refrigerated.

INDEX

All recipe titles are listed in French and English. Ingredients are indexed in English only.